CW01211615

OCR SHP GCSE

THE FIRST CRUSADE c.1070–1100

RACHEL FOSTER
KATH GOUDIE

SERIES EDITORS:
Jamie Byrom and Michael Riley

DYNAMIC LEARNING

HODDER EDUCATION
AN HACHETTE UK COMPANY

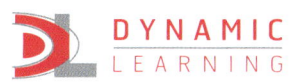

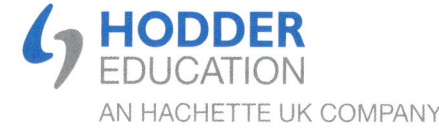

The Schools History Project

Set up in 1972 to bring new life to history for school students, the Schools History Project has been based at Leeds Trinity University since 1978. SHP continues to play an innovatory role in history education based on its six principles:

- Making history meaningful for young people
- Engaging in historical enquiry
- Developing broad and deep knowledge
- Studying the historic environment
- Promoting diversity and inclusion
- Supporting rigorous and enjoyable learning

These principles are embedded in the resources which SHP produces in partnership with Hodder Education to support history at Key Stage 3, GCSE (SHP OCR B) and A level. The Schools History Project contributes to national debate about school history. It strives to challenge, support and inspire teachers through its published resources, conferences and website: http://www.schoolshistoryproject.org.uk

This resource is endorsed by OCR for use with specification OCR Level 1/2 GCSE (9–1) in History B (Schools History Project) (J411). In order to gain OCR endorsement, this resource has undergone an independent quality check. Any references to assessment and/or assessment preparation are the publisher's interpretation of the specification requirements and are not endorsed by OCR. OCR recommends that a range of teaching and learning resources are used in preparing learners for assessment. OCR has not paid for the production of this resource, nor does OCR receive any royalties from its sale. For more information about the endorsement process, please visit the OCR website, www.ocr.co.uk.

The publishers thank OCR for permission to use specimen exam questions on pages 101–104 from OCR's GCSE (9–1) History B (Schools History Project) © OCR 2016. OCR have neither seen nor commented upon any model answers or exam guidance related to these questions.

The wording and sentence structure of some written sources have been adapted and simplified to make them accessible to all pupils while faithfully preserving the sense of the original

Every effort has been made to trace all copyright holders, but if any have been inadvertently overlooked, the Publishers will be pleased to make the necessary arrangements at the first opportunity.

Although every effort has been made to ensure that website addresses are correct at time of going to press, Hodder Education cannot be held responsible for the content of any website mentioned in this book. It is sometimes possible to find a relocated web page by typing in the address of the home page for a website in the URL window of your browser.

Hachette UK's policy is to use papers that are natural, renewable and recyclable products and made from wood grown in sustainable forests. The logging and manufacturing processes are expected to conform to the environmental regulations of the country of origin.

Orders: please contact Bookpoint Ltd, 130 Park Drive, Milton Park, Abingdon, Oxon OX14 4SE. Telephone: (44) 01235 827720. Fax: (44) 01235 400454. Email education@bookpoint.co.uk Lines are open from 9 a.m. to 5 p.m., Monday to Saturday, with a 24-hour message answering service. You can also order through our website: www.hoddereducation.co.uk

ISBN: 9781471861048

© Rachel Foster and Kath Goudie 2017

First published in 2017 by
Hodder Education,
An Hachette UK Company
Carmelite House
50 Victoria Embankment
London EC4Y 0DZ

www.hoddereducation.co.uk

Impression number   10 9 8 7 6 5 4 3 2 1

Year   2019 2018 2017

All rights reserved. Apart from any use permitted under UK copyright law, no part of this publication may be reproduced or transmitted in any form or by any means, electronic or mechanical, including photocopying and recording, or held within any information storage and retrieval system, without permission in writing from the publisher or under licence from the Copyright Licensing Agency Limited. Further details of such licences (for reprographic reproduction) may be obtained from the Copyright Licensing Agency Limited, Saffron House, 6–10 Kirby Street, London EC1N 8TS.

Cover photo © North Wind Picture Archives/Alamy Stock Photo

Illustrations by White-Thompson Publishing Ltd, Barking Dog

Typeset by White-Thomson Publishing Ltd

Printed in Italy

A catalogue record for this title is available from the British Library.

CONTENTS

	Introduction	2
	Making the most of this book	
1	**Changing worlds**	8
	Where do the origins of the First Crusade lie?	
	Closer look 1: Finding out about the First Crusade	
2	**Responses**	26
	What was so remarkable about the start of the First Crusade?	
	Closer look 2: Robert Curthose, a Norman knight	
3	**Into the Muslim world**	44
	How well did the crusaders deal with the challenges of Asia Minor?	
	Closer look 3: The art of siege warfare	
4	**'The greatest test'**	62
	Why did it take the crusaders so long to capture the city of Antioch?	
	Closer look 4: The Byzantine–crusader relationship: explaining the behaviour of Tatikios	
5	**To the Holy City**	80
	How did the crusaders establish the Kingdom of Jerusalem?	
	Closer look 5: Islamic perspectives on the First Crusade	
	Preparing for the examination	98
	Glossary	106
	Index	108
	Acknowledgements	110

INTRODUCTION

Making the most of this book

● Where this book fits into your GCSE history course

The course

The GCSE history course you are following is made up of five different studies. These are shown in the table below. For each type of study you will follow one option. We have highlighted the option that this particular book helps you with.

OCR SHP GCSE B

(Choose one option from each section)

Paper 1 1¾ hours	**British thematic study** ● The People's Health ● Crime and Punishment ● Migrants to Britain	**20%**
	British depth study ● The Norman Conquest ● Elizabethan England ● Britain in Peace and War	**20%**
Paper 2 1 hour	**History around us** ● Any site that meets the given criteria	**20%**
Paper 3 1¾ hours	**World period study** ● Viking Expansion ● The Mughal Empire ● The Making of America	**20%**
	World depth study ● The First Crusade  ● Aztecs and the Spanish Conquest ● Living Under Nazi Rule	**20%**

The world depth study

The world depth study focuses on a traumatic short period in world history when different cultures or ideologies were in conflict. It encourages you to engage with many rich, contemporary sources and the different interpretations of historians. As you do this you will learn about the nature of historical evidence and how history is constructed.

Introduction

As the table shows, you will be examined on your knowledge and understanding of the world depth study as part of Paper 3. You can find out more about that on pages 98–105 at the back of the book.

Here is exactly what the specification requires for this depth study.

The First Crusade, c.1070–1100

The specification divides this period into five sections:

Sections	Learners should study the following content:
Origins c.1070–1095	• The Islamic world, including its diversity and its relations with Christians • Pressures on the Byzantine Empire • Latin Christendom and the power of the papacy
Responses November 1095 to December 1096	• Urban II and the preaching of the First Crusade • Joining the First Crusade: who went and why • The People's Crusade and the challenges it faced
Into Asia Minor December 1096 to October 1097	• Alexios I and his negotiations with the crusade leaders • The siege of Nicaea and the Battle of Dorylaeum: the nature of Christian and Muslim warfare • The journey across Asia Minor: physical challenges and disunity among the leadership
Antioch October 1097 to June 1098	• The siege by the crusaders • The capture of Antioch: rivalries, strategies and atrocities • The events of June and the defeat of Kerbogha
Jerusalem	• Disputes, delays and the journey to Jerusalem • The capture of Jerusalem: preparations, tactics and the sack of the city • The establishment of the Kingdom of Jerusalem and the Muslim response

You need to understand the interplay between these forces that shaped the First Crusade:

- Political
- Military
- Economic
- Social
- Religious
- Cultural

You also need to understand:

- the main events of the First Crusade
- the diverse lives and experiences of Muslims and Christians at that time.

In addition, you should be able to:

- engage with a range of historical sources that shed light on the First Crusade
- understand different interpretations of aspects of the First Crusade.

The next two pages show how this book works.

How this book works

The rest of this book (from pages 8 to 97) is carefully arranged to match what the specification requires. It does this through the following features:

Enquiries

The book is largely taken up with five 'enquiries'. Each enquiry sets you a challenge in the form of an overarching question.

The first two pages of the enquiry set up the challenge and give you a clear sense of what you will need to do to work out your answer to the main question. You will find the instructions set out in 'The Enquiry' box, on a blue background, as in this example.

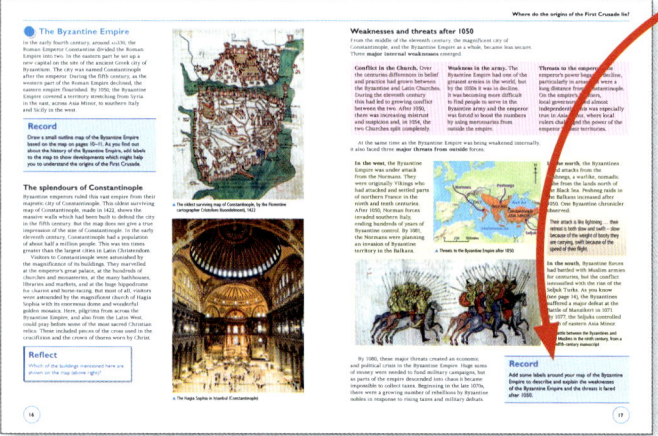

Record tasks

From that point, the enquiry is divided into three sections. These match the bullet points shown in the specification on page 3. You can tell when you are starting a new section as it will start with a large coloured heading like the one shown here. Throughout each section there are 'Record' tasks, where you will be asked to record ideas and information that will help you make up your mind about the overarching enquiry question later on. You can see an example of these 'Record' instructions here. They will always be in blue text with blue lines above and below them.

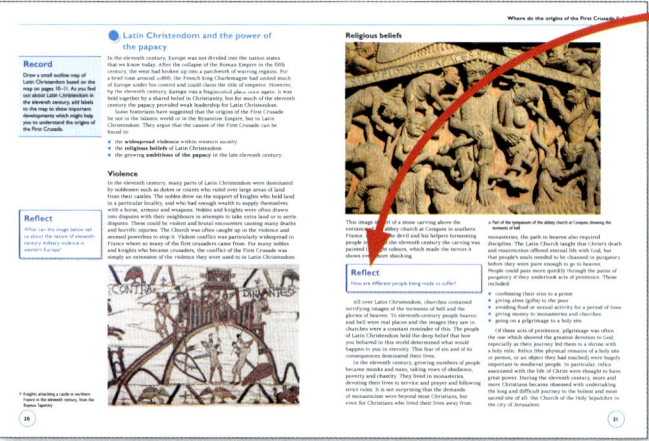

Reflect tasks

At regular intervals we will set a 'Reflect' task to prompt you to think carefully about what you are reading. They will look like the examples shown here. These Reflect tasks help you to check that what you are reading is making sense and to see how it connects with what you have already learned. You do not need to write down the ideas that you think of when you 'reflect', but the ideas you get may help you when you reach the next Record instruction.

Introduction

Review tasks

Each enquiry ends by asking you to review what you have been learning and use it to answer the overarching question in some way. Sometimes you simply answer that one question. Sometimes you will need to do two or three tasks that each tackle some aspect of the main question. The important point is that you should be able to use the ideas and evidence you have been building up through the enquiry to support your answer.

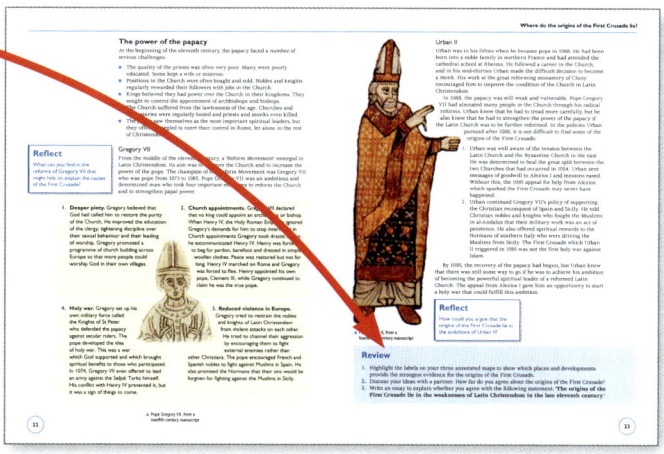

Closer looks

Between the enquiries you will find pages that provide a 'closer look' at some aspect of the theme or period you are studying. These will often give you a chance to find out more about the issue you have just been studying in the previous enquiry, although they may sometimes look ahead to the next enquiry.

We may not include any tasks within these 'closer looks' but, as you read them, keep thinking of what they add to your knowledge and understanding. We think they add some intriguing insights.

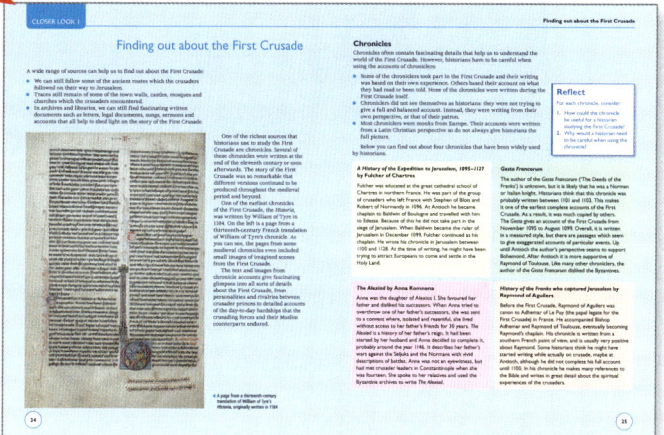

One very important final point

We have chosen enquiry questions that should help you get to the really important issues at the heart of each period you study, but you need to remember that the examiners will almost certainly ask you different questions when you take your GCSE. Don't simply rely on the notes you made to answer the enquiry questions we gave you. We give you advice on how to tackle the examination and the different sorts of question you will face on pages 98 to 105.

The First Crusade

◀ An illustration of the departure of Godfrey of Bouillon in the summer of 1096. From a thirteenth-century edition of William of Tyre's *History of the Kingdom of Jerusalem*, c.1184

Until 1095, Godfrey of Bouillon lived as a minor nobleman in northern France. Then everything changed. In 1096, Godfrey and tens of thousands of other Christians left their homes in western Europe and set off on a 2000-mile journey to the Holy Land. Their expedition would later become known as the First Crusade. The crusaders had been inspired by Pope Urban II's call for a Holy War to recapture the city of Jerusalem from its Muslim rulers who, at the time, were known in Europe as Saracens.

Before they left, the crusaders prayed for God's protection, but few of them could have imagined the challenges that lay ahead. Godfrey and the other leaders often disagreed over important decisions. On their three-year journey to the Holy Land, many crusaders were killed in hard-fought battles and sieges. Thousands of others died of disease and hunger. At one point, some crusaders were so desperate for food that they tried to stay alive by eating their own shoes.

By the time the crusaders reached Jerusalem in July 1099, only a few thousand remained. But the survivors were convinced that retaking Jerusalem would earn them the reward of eternal paradise in heaven. The crusaders attacked Jerusalem on 14 July. On the second day of fighting, Godfrey of Bouillon led the crusaders over Jerusalem's 15-metre high walls. The massacre that followed was deeply shocking, even by the standards of the Middle Ages.

Picturing the First Crusade

No pictures of the First Crusade survive from the time, but from the later Middle Ages until the present, artists have used written accounts to imagine particular events from the crusade. In 1184, William of Tyre wrote the first history of the Kingdom of Jerusalem. The picture above was produced for a thirteenth-century edition of William of Tyre's book. It is a medieval artist's interpretation of the moment when Godfrey of Bouillon and his followers set out on the First Crusade.

Reflect

How did the medieval artist try to portray the emotion of this moment?

Introduction

Pictures are often powerful interpretations of history because they fix ideas in the popular imagination. In the nineteenth century, when many European countries were building empires across the world, rulers often looked back to the First Crusade for inspiration. They saw it as a glorious and heroic event in the history of their nation. Nineteenth-century artists produced romanticised paintings of the First Crusade which emphasised the heroism of those involved.

The painting below was produced in 1847 by the French artist Émile Signol. It shows Godfrey of Bouillon and the other crusaders rejoicing in victory after taking Jerusalem.

Reflect

How did Émile Signol portray this event as a glorious moment?

▼ *Taking of Jerusalem by the Crusaders.* A painting by the French artist Émile Signol, 1847

As you find out about the events of the First Crusade in this book, you will encounter a range of visual and other interpretations. These help us understand how the First Crusade has been viewed over time. They also demonstrate how some interpretations can distort the past and reinforce dangerous divisions between the West and the Islamic world. The most helpful interpretations for understanding the First Crusade are based on the careful analysis of historical sources. Together these can reveal the real and complex lives of people caught up in the events – their hopes, struggles, fears and joys. That's what makes the study of the First Crusade so fascinating.

Changing worlds

Where do the origins of the First Crusade lie?

Jerusalem is one of the most beautiful, holy and disputed cities in the world. Its history stretches back thousands of years. It was here that King Solomon built the first Jewish temple in 950BC. Around AD33, Jesus was crucified here. In the fourth century, the Church of the Holy Sepulchre was built close to the site of the crucifixion and of Christ's tomb. In the Middle Ages, Jerusalem was the centre of the Christian world. Pilgrims flocked to the city to pray at its holy sites.

In AD638, followers of a new faith, Islam, captured Jerusalem. The Muslims built a holy shrine on top of the Temple Mount for they believed that it was from here that their Prophet Muhammad had ascended to heaven on his miraculous Night Journey. The shrine is known as the Dome of the Rock. Centuries later it was given the golden dome which you can see in the photograph below.

The Muslims accepted Jesus as a prophet and did not destroy the Church of the Holy Sepulchre. For over 400 years they allowed Christians to live in Jerusalem and the Holy Land surrounding the city. Christian pilgrims continued to visit the sacred sites. Then, at the end of the eleventh century, all this changed. A group of Muslims known as the Seljuk Turks took control of Jerusalem. The expansion of the Seljuk Turks placed Christianity in the east under threat. The result was the First Crusade.

▼ A panorama of Jerusalem

Where do the origins of the First Crusade lie?

As you learned on page 6, it was 1096 when many thousands of Christians set off from Europe on this crusade. They were united in their intense desire to bring Jerusalem back under Christian control. Their journey would take three years. Along the way they experienced hardship, hunger and the horrors of war. When they eventually captured Jerusalem in 1099, the crusaders unleashed a terrible slaughter and the blood of Muslims and Jews ran through the streets of the historic holy city.

The Enquiry

Why the First Crusade happened when it did is a question that fascinates historians. The causes of the First Crusade are complex and historians disagree about when and where the origins of the First Crusade lie. In this enquiry you will develop your own view about the origins of the First Crusade. To do this you will find out about the history of three different areas of the world:

1. the Islamic world
2. the Byzantine Empire
3. Latin Christendom.

As you learn about each area you will label a map to show the developments that might help to explain the origins of the First Crusade. At the end of the enquiry you will use your three annotated maps to challenge a particular interpretation about where the origins of the First Crusade lie.

The world of the First Crusade

This map shows western Europe and the Mediterranean around the year 1070. You may know some of the places on the map, but the shaded areas seem unfamiliar to our modern minds. These were the three big powers which dominated this part of the world in the late eleventh century:

- the Islamic world
- the Byzantine Empire
- Latin Christendom.

Reflect

Read the text panels about each of the three big powers.

1. What tensions can you find within and between the powers c.1070?
2. How do you think any of these might have helped to cause the First Crusade?

Latin Christendom

In 1070, Europe was a fragmented patchwork of warring kingdoms and regions. It was a less advanced power than either the Islamic world or the Byzantine Empire, and its cities were much smaller. In Rome, the pope was the spiritual leader of Latin Christendom, but his position was insecure. In the eleventh century, people from Latin Christendom travelled to Jerusalem on pilgrimage, but by 1070 the Seljuk Turks were making this increasingly difficult.

▲ Map of Europe, the Near East and North Africa, c.1070

Where do the origins of the First Crusade lie?

The Byzantine Empire

This was the remaining eastern part of what had once been the Roman Empire. From its magnificent capital, Constantinople, the Byzantine Empire stretched west to the Balkans and east across Asia Minor. From the middle of the eleventh century, the Byzantine Empire came under increasing pressure, particularly from the Seljuk Turks who captured land from the Byzantines in the eastern part of Asia Minor. The Byzantine Emperor in Constantinople needed help from people beyond his empire.

The Islamic world

In the seventh century, Islam spread rapidly from its original home in Arabia. In AD 638 Muslim warriors captured the city of Jerusalem and the surrounding Holy Land from the Christian Byzantines. By the eleventh century, the Islamic world stretched from as far as India in the east to al-Andalus (now southern Spain) in the west. But the Islamic Empire was divided. It was split between the Abbasids based in Baghdad and the Fatimids based in Cairo. In addition, a new tribe of Islamic warriors, the Seljuk Turks, was threatening the Byzantine Empire in the east.

The Islamic world

Record

Draw a small outline map of the Islamic world based on the map on pages 10–11. As you find out about the history of the Islamic world, add labels around the map to show important developments which might help us to understand the origins of the First Crusade.

Islamic expansion

Nearly five centuries before the First Crusade, a new religion had emerged in southern Arabia: Islam. Founded by the Prophet Muhammad between AD610 and AD618, the Muslim faith spread with incredible speed. Following the Prophet's death in AD632, Muslim warriors quickly conquered Arabia. In AD638, they moved into Palestine where they captured the city of Jerusalem from the Byzantine Christians.

Jerusalem was Islam's third holiest site after Mecca and Medina. In AD692, on top of the rocky outcrop from where it was believed the Prophet began his miraculous Night Journey to heaven and back, the Muslims built the holy shrine known as the Dome of the Rock. Nearby, they later built the Aqsa Mosque.

Islam dominated Jerusalem and the Holy Land for the next 400 years. For much of this time, Muslim rulers allowed the Christian and Jewish populations to continue in their faiths as long as they paid a special tax and did not try to convert Muslims. The Muslim rulers also permitted pilgrims from Europe to visit the sacred Christian sites in Jerusalem and Palestine.

During the eighth and ninth centuries, Islam spread with astonishing speed from its early conquests in Arabia and Palestine:

- **In the east,** Muslim warriors conquered the lands that are now Iraq and Iran.
- **In the north,** they moved into Syria and pushed into the Byzantine Empire.
- **In the west,** much of Egypt, North Africa and Spain fell under Muslim control.

By the end of the ninth century, the Muslims had even seized the Byzantine island of Sicily. There, they were less than 300 miles from the centre of Latin Christendom in Rome.

Reflect

1. In what ways could you argue that the origin of the First Crusade lies in seventh-century Jerusalem?
2. What made a Christian attempt to take back control of Jerusalem and the Holy Land unlikely in the four centuries after 638?

▶ The Dome of the Rock, Jerusalem

The achievements of the Islamic world

In the ninth century AD, the Islamic world covered a vast territory stretching from India in the east to al-Andalus in the west. United by religion, the Arabic language and trade, a rich Islamic culture emerged which was far more advanced than Latin Christendom and the Byzantine Empire. At the centre of the Islamic world was a family dynasty called the Abbasids who ruled from their huge circular city of Baghdad (see map on pages 10–11).

Baghdad had trade links with the distant lands of Africa, Byzantium, India and China. It was a city of books and learning where scholars from all over the Islamic world came to study ancient texts. Ninth-century Baghdad was a fabulously wealthy city, famous for the glassware, ceramics and textiles produced in its workshops. When Byzantine ambassadors visited the Abbasid caliph (ruler), they marvelled at the thousands of beautiful silks hanging in his palace at the centre of Baghdad.

By the end of the ninth century, other great cities such as Damascus, Mecca, Cairo and Cordoba were also important centres of production and trade (see map on pages 10–11). Muslim merchants from these cities traded in spices, silks and other luxury goods. They helped to spread wealth and ideas across the Islamic world.

▲ An Abbasid library, from a thirteenth-century document

Divisions

In the second half of the tenth century, the Abbasids began to lose their hold on power. For three centuries, there had been a deep division in the Islamic world between two groups:

- **Sunni Muslims,** who defended the right of the Abbasid caliphs to be the leaders of Islam
- **Shi'ite Muslims,** who believed that only the descendants of Ali (Muhammad's cousin and son-in-law) had the right to rule.

In 969, a Shi'ite dynasty known as the Fatimids broke free from Abbasid control and set up a rival caliphate in Cairo. The Fatimids soon controlled Egypt and Palestine, including Jerusalem.

In 1009, a mentally deranged Fatimid ruler, Caliph Hakim, ended the toleration of Christians in the Holy Land and ordered the destruction of the Church of the Holy Sepulchre. Pilgrimages to Jerusalem stopped, and there was much anger across the Christian world. Fatimid rulers who came after Hakim restored relations with Christians and invited the Byzantines to rebuild the Church of the Holy Sepulchre. Tensions eased, but a new Islamic threat to the Byzantines developed in the eleventh century – the Seljuk Turks.

The Seljuk Turks

The Seljuk Turks were a tribe from central Asia who had converted to Islam in the tenth century. By the 1040s, these fierce mounted warriors had moved into the area we now call Iraq. In 1055, the Seljuks seized Baghdad from the Abbasids. Their leader took control from the caliph and gave himself the title of sultan. The Seljuks were the new rulers of Sunni Islam. They fought to expand their territory still further, and by 1071 they had taken Jerusalem from the Fatimids.

The Byzantines also suffered from the rise of the Seljuk Turks. Some of the Seljuks were determined to take new lands in the Byzantine Empire. In 1071, they crushed the Byzantine army at the Battle of Manzikert. The Byzantine emperor was captured by the Seljuks and was forced to hand over large parts of his territory before his release. The eastern regions of the Byzantine Empire were now under Seljuk control. It was a devastating blow for the Byzantines.

Crises in the 1090s

Seljuk power weakened in the mid-1090s. Following the sultan's death in 1092, his two sons fought to become the next ruler and Seljuk rule collapsed into civil war. In Egypt, the Fatimids were also weakened when their caliph died in 1094. It is unlikely that news of the difficulties faced by the Islamic world in the 1090s reached Europe, but the First Crusade could not have begun at a worse time for the Muslims.

> **Reflect**
>
> This modern painting shows the victorious Seljuk army after the Battle of Manzikert. How has the artist portrayed Manzikert as a great victory for the Seljuks?

▼ A modern painting of the Battle of Manzikert in the Istanbul Military Museum

Troubles in Sicily and al-Andalus

Some historians think that the First Crusade had its origins not in developments in the lands around the eastern Mediterranean, but in the far west of the Islamic world: Sicily and al-Andalus (Muslim Spain). They point out that several Muslim chroniclers saw the First Crusade as part of a Mediterranean-wide struggle which was focused on Sicily and al-Andalus, as well as on Jerusalem.

> **From *The Perfect Work of History* by Ibn al-Athir, twelfth century**
> The first appearance of the power of the Franks [Latin Christians] and the extension of their rule – namely, attacks directed against Islamic territory and the conquest of some of these lands – occurred in 1085 when they took Toledo and other cities in Islamic Spain [al-Andalus].
> Then, in 1091, they attacked and conquered the Island of Sicily; from there they extended their reach as far as the coast of North Africa, where they captured some places. The conquests [in North Africa] were won back, but they took possession of other lands as you will see.

The 'other lands' mentioned by Ibn al-Athir were the territories in Syria and Palestine which were conquered by the first crusaders. Ibn al-Athir clearly saw the First Crusade as part of a wider struggle which included the western Mediterranean.

> **Reflect**
> According to Ibn al-Athir, what dates and events are important in understanding the origins of the First Crusade?

In fact, the troubles in Sicily and al-Andalus had begun earlier than Ibn al-Athir suggested:

Sicily

By the middle of the eleventh century, the Fatimid grip on Sicily had weakened and the island was split between several competing Muslim warlords. In 1061, Norman knights, encouraged by the pope, made the short crossing from southern Italy and attacked the port of Messina on the east coast of Sicily. The Normans expected to conquer Sicily quickly, but Muslim opposition on the island meant that it took many years. In 1071, the Normans captured Palermo, the Muslim capital of Sicily. By 1090, they had taken control of the whole island. Muslim rule in Sicily had finally come to an end.

al-Andalus

From the 1030s, al-Andalus was divided by civil war. Rival groups of Muslim warlords fought each other for control of territory. The Christian rulers of northern Spain saw this as a good opportunity to intervene. At the same time as the Normans slowly conquered and settled Sicily, Spanish lords and their knights gradually took back much of al-Andalus into Christian hands. In 1085, the city and Kingdom of Toledo fell to the Christians. Its main mosque was soon converted into a cathedral. The conquest of Toledo sent shock waves through the Islamic world.

> **Reflect**
> How do you think developments in Sicily and al-Andalus might have contributed to the origins of the First Crusade?

> **Record**
> Add more labels to your map to show important developments which might help you to understand the origins of the First Crusade.

The Byzantine Empire

In the early fourth century, around AD330, the Roman Emperor Constantine divided the Roman Empire into two. In the eastern part he set up a new capital on the site of the ancient Greek city of Byzantium. The city was named Constantinople after the emperor. During the fifth century, as the western part of the Roman Empire declined, the eastern empire flourished. By 1050, the Byzantine Empire covered a territory stretching from Syria in the east, across Asia Minor, to southern Italy and Sicily in the west.

Record
Draw a small outline map of the Byzantine Empire based on the map on pages 10–11. As you find out about the history of the Byzantine Empire, add labels to the map to show developments which might help you to understand the origins of the First Crusade.

The splendours of Constantinople

Byzantine emperors ruled this vast empire from their majestic city of Constantinople. This oldest surviving map of Constantinople, made in 1422, shows the massive walls which had been built to defend the city in the fifth century. But the map does not give a true impression of the size of Constantinople. In the early eleventh century, Constantinople had a population of about half a million people. This was ten times greater than the largest cities in Latin Christendom.

Visitors to Constantinople were astonished by the magnificence of its buildings. They marvelled at the emperor's great palace, at the hundreds of churches and monasteries, at the many bathhouses, libraries and markets, and at the huge hippodrome for chariot and horse-racing. But most of all, visitors were astounded by the magnificent church of Hagia Sophia with its enormous dome and wonderful golden mosaics. Here, pilgrims from across the Byzantine Empire, and also from the Latin West, could pray before some of the most sacred Christian relics. These included pieces of the cross used in the crucifixion and the crown of thorns worn by Christ.

Reflect
Which of the buildings mentioned here are shown on the map (above right)?

▲ The oldest surviving map of Constantinople, by the Florentine cartographer Cristoforo Buondelmonti, 1422

▲ The Hagia Sophia in Istanbul (Constantinople)

Where do the origins of the First Crusade lie?

Weaknesses and threats after 1050

From the middle of the eleventh century, the magnificent city of Constantinople, and the Byzantine Empire as a whole, became less secure. Three **major internal weaknesses** emerged:

Conflict in the Church. Over the centuries differences in belief and practice had grown between the Byzantine and Latin Churches. During the eleventh century this had led to growing conflict between the two. After 1050, there was increasing mistrust and suspicion and, in 1054, the two Churches split completely.	**Weakness in the army.** The Byzantine Empire had one of the greatest armies in the world, but by the 1050s it was in decline. It was becoming more difficult to find people to serve in the Byzantine army and the emperor was forced to boost the numbers by using mercenaries from outside the empire.	**Threats to the emperor.** The emperor's power began to decline, particularly in areas that were a long distance from Constantinople. On the empire's frontiers, local governors ruled almost independently. This was especially true in Asia Minor, where local rulers challenged the power of the emperor in their territories.

At the same time as the Byzantine Empire was being weakened internally, it also faced three **major threats from outside** forces:

In the west, the Byzantine Empire was under attack from the Normans. They were originally Vikings who had attacked and settled parts of northern France in the ninth and tenth centuries. After 1050, Norman forces invaded southern Italy, ending hundreds of years of Byzantine control. By 1081, the Normans were planning an invasion of Byzantine territory in the Balkans.

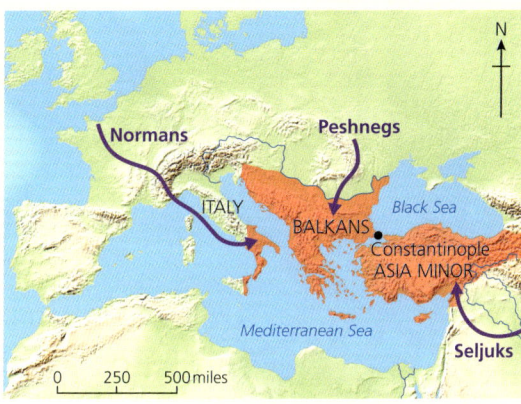
▲ Threats to the Byzantine Empire after 1050

In the north, the Byzantines faced attacks from the Peshnegs, a warlike, nomadic tribe from the lands north of the Black Sea. Peshneg raids in the Balkans increased after 1050. One Byzantine chronicler observed:

> Their attack is like lightning ... their retreat is both slow and swift – slow because of the weight of booty they are carrying, swift because of the speed of their flight.

In the south, Byzantine forces had battled with Muslim armies for centuries, but the conflict intensified with the rise of the Seljuk Turks. As you know (see page 14), the Byzantines suffered a major defeat at the Battle of Manzikert in 1071. By 1077, the Seljuks controlled much of eastern Asia Minor.

◀ A battle between the Byzantines and the Muslims in the ninth century, from a twelfth-century manuscript

By 1080, these major threats created an economic and political crisis in the Byzantine Empire. Huge sums of money were needed to fund military campaigns, but as parts of the empire descended into chaos it became impossible to collect taxes. Beginning in the late 1070s, there were a growing number of rebellions by Byzantine nobles in response to rising taxes and military defeats.

Record

Add some labels around your map of the Byzantine Empire to describe and explain the weaknesses of the Byzantine Empire and the threats it faced after 1050.

17

The new emperor, Alexios I

▲ A twelfth-century mosaic portrait of Alexios I in Hagia Sophia, Istanbul (Constantinople). Apart from his portrait on coins, this is only one of two images of Alexios known to exist

The man who had to deal with the weaknesses and threats facing the Byzantine Empire after 1081 was Alexios Komnenos. In February of that year, this brilliant military commander from a respected Byzantine family seized power in a military coup. The new emperor was only 24 years old. His daughter, Anna Komnena, later described him:

From Anna Komnena, *The Alexiad*, c.1146

He reminded one of a fiery whirlwind … His dark eyebrows were curved, and beneath them the gaze of his eyes was both terrible and kind. His broad shoulders, muscular arms and deep chest, all on a heroic scale, invariably commanded the wonder and delight of the people. He radiated beauty and grace and dignity and an unapproachable majesty.

Unlike some previous emperors, Alexios disliked luxury. He was famous for his modesty and piety. After he seized the throne he slept on a stone floor in a hair shirt to atone for his soldiers' behaviour. Shunning the Byzantine elites, he invited the poor to dine with him in the palace and spent his evenings reading the Bible, alongside his equally devout wife.

Recovery, 1081–90

Alexios I turned his back on the life of luxury enjoyed by previous emperors in Constantinople. Instead, he focused on military affairs. With the help of mercenaries from Latin Christendom and the Islamic world, he was able to overcome two of the three threats facing the Byzantine Empire:

- In 1081, the Normans launched their attack on the Balkans, inflicting a crushing defeat on the Byzantine army. Emperor Alexios himself only avoided capture after a high-speed chase on horseback. However, in the late 1080s, Alexios succeeded in driving the Normans out of the Balkans. They remained, however, a continuing threat to the Byzantines.
- In 1090, a vast group of Peshnegs invaded the Byzantine Empire from the north and reached the walls of Constantinople. Emperor Alexios led out his army to face them and won a stunning victory. Never again would they threaten the Byzantine Empire.

By 1090, with the Normans forced out of the Balkans and the Peshnegs completely destroyed, Alexios had turned around the fortunes of the Byzantine Empire in the north and west. But the Seljuk Turks in the south would prove a greater challenge.

Crisis, 1090–95

In the 1080s, while Alexios had been fighting in the north and west of his empire, Turkish warlords had continued to threaten Asia Minor. The only way that Alexios had been able to defend his territory had been to strike a deal with the Seljuk sultan of Baghdad, Malik Shah. The sultan provided Alexios with troops and drove Turkish raiders from Byzantine lands. In return, the Seljuk Turks were lavished with gifts and were given control of the great Byzantine cities of Nicaea and Antioch, which they ruled on the emperor's behalf.

For a while, a fragile stability was restored. Then, in 1092, the situation collapsed when Sultan Malik Shah suddenly died. This increased the pressure on the Byzantine Empire as different Turkish warlords rushed to grab land in Anatolia. By 1094, many important coastal towns had fallen and Byzantine control of much of Anatolia had collapsed.

As the situation in Anatolia worsened, Byzantine nobles became increasingly critical of Alexios. In 1094, he narrowly avoided being assassinated by a rival. While fighting in the Balkans, a plot was hatched to murder him as he slept in his tent. The would-be murderer, a rival to the throne, failed to go through with it when he realised the emperor's wife was with him. He was arrested and tortured, revealing that the plot was widely supported by senior members of the army, government and even Alexios's own family. After sharing these alarming secrets, he was blinded, a punishment that was traditionally used on plotters at the Byzantine court.

Alexios had to re-assert his authority as emperor. His response was to send an envoy to the pope with an appeal for help against the Seljuk Turks. He believed that victory against the Turks and the recovery of lost Byzantine lands would silence his critics. It was Pope Urban's response to Alexios' appeal that triggered the First Crusade.

The crisis in the Byzantine Empire was so great by 1095 that some historians are convinced we should look for the origins of the First Crusade in the east rather than the west. In 2012, the historian Peter Frankopan wrote a book called *The First Crusade: The Call from the East*. He argued that the true origins of the First Crusade lie in what was happening in the Byzantine Empire at the end of the eleventh century.

▲ The blinding of a general who had plotted against the Byzantine emperor in 919. From a twelfth-century Greek manuscript.

Reflect

Which of the labels you have been making as you worked through pages 16–19 provide the strongest points in support of Peter Frankopan's view?

Record

Add more labels to your map to summarise the main developments in the Byzantine Empire after 1090. Use a different colour from your first set of labels.

Latin Christendom and the power of the papacy

In the eleventh century, Europe was not divided into the nation states that we know today. After the collapse of the Roman Empire in the fifth century, the west had broken up into a patchwork of warring regions. For a brief time around AD800, the French king Charlemagne had united much of Europe under his control and could claim the title of emperor. However, by the eleventh century, Europe was a fragmented place once again. It was held together by a shared belief in Christianity, but for much of the eleventh century the papacy provided weak leadership for Latin Christendom.

Some historians have suggested that the origins of the First Crusade lie not in the Islamic world or in the Byzantine Empire, but in Latin Christendom. They argue that the causes of the First Crusade can be found in:

- the **widespread violence** within western society
- the **religious beliefs** of Latin Christendom
- the growing **ambitions of the papacy** in the late eleventh century.

Violence

In the eleventh century, many parts of Latin Christendom were dominated by noblemen such as dukes or counts who ruled over large areas of land from their castles. The nobles drew on the support of knights who held land in a particular locality, and who had enough wealth to supply themselves with a horse, armour and weapons. Nobles and knights were often drawn into disputes with their neighbours in attempts to take extra land or to settle disputes. These could be violent and brutal encounters causing many deaths and horrific injuries. The Church was often caught up in the violence and seemed powerless to stop it. Violent conflict was particularly widespread in France where so many of the first crusaders came from. For many nobles and knights who became crusaders, the conflict of the First Crusade was simply an extension of the violence they were used to in Latin Christendom.

> ### Record
> Draw a small outline map of Latin Christendom based on the map on pages 10–11. As you find out about Latin Christendom in the eleventh century, add labels to the map to show important developments which might help you to understand the origins of the First Crusade.

> ### Reflect
> What can the image below tell us about the nature of eleventh-century military violence in western Europe?

▶ Knights attacking a castle in northern France in the eleventh century, from the Bayeux Tapestry

Religious beliefs

▲ Part of the tympanum of the abbey church at Conques showing the torments of hell

This image is part of a stone carving above the entrance of the abbey church at Conques in southern France. It shows the devil and his helpers tormenting people in hell. In the eleventh century the carving was painted in bright colours, which made the terrors it shows even more shocking.

> ## Reflect
> How are different people being made to suffer?

All over Latin Christendom, churches contained terrifying images of the torments of hell and the glories of heaven. To eleventh-century people heaven and hell were real places and the images they saw in churches were a constant reminder of this. The people of Latin Christendom held the deep belief that how you behaved in this world determined what would happen to you in eternity. This fear of sin and of its consequences dominated their lives.

In the eleventh century, growing numbers of people became monks and nuns, taking vows of obedience, poverty and chastity. They lived in monasteries, devoting their lives to service and prayer and following strict rules. It is not surprising that the demands of monasticism were beyond most Christians, but even for Christians who lived their lives away from monasteries, the path to heaven also required discipline. The Latin Church taught that Christ's death and resurrection offered eternal life with God, but that people's souls needed to be cleansed in purgatory before they were pure enough to go to heaven. People could pass more quickly through the pains of purgatory if they undertook acts of penitence. These included:

- confessing their sins to a priest
- giving alms (gifts) to the poor
- avoiding food or sexual activity for a period of time
- giving money to monasteries and churches
- going on a pilgrimage to a holy site.

Of these acts of penitence, pilgrimage was often the one which showed the greatest devotion to God, especially as their journey led them to a shrine with a holy relic. Relics (the physical remains of a holy site or person, or an object they had touched) were hugely important to medieval people. In particular, relics associated with the life of Christ were thought to have great power. During the eleventh century, more and more Christians became obsessed with undertaking the long and difficult journey to the holiest and most sacred site of all: the Church of the Holy Sepulchre in the city of Jerusalem.

The power of the papacy

At the beginning of the eleventh century, the papacy faced a number of serious challenges:

- The quality of the priests was often very poor. Many were poorly educated. Some kept a wife or mistress.
- Positions in the Church were often bought and sold. Nobles and knights regularly rewarded their followers with jobs in the Church.
- Kings believed they had power over the Church in their kingdoms. They sought to control the appointment of archbishops and bishops.
- The Church suffered from the lawlessness of the age. Churches and monasteries were regularly looted and priests and monks even killed.
- The popes saw themselves as the most important spiritual leaders, but they often struggled to exert their control in Rome, let alone in the rest of Christendom.

Gregory VII

From the middle of the eleventh century, a 'Reform Movement' emerged in Latin Christendom. Its aim was to improve the Church and to increase the power of the pope. The champion of the Reform Movement was Gregory VII who was pope from 1073 to 1085. Pope Gregory VII was an ambitious and determined man who took four important measures to reform the Church and to strengthen papal power.

> **Reflect**
>
> What can you find in the reforms of Gregory VII that might help to explain the causes of the First Crusade?

1. **Deeper piety.** Gregory believed that God had called him to restore the purity of the Church. He improved the education of the clergy, tightening discipline over their sexual behaviour and their leading of worship. Gregory promoted a programme of church building across Europe so that more people could worship God in their own villages.

2. **Church appointments.** Gregory VII declared that no king could appoint an archbishop or bishop. When Henry IV, the Holy Roman Emperor, ignored Gregory's demands for him to stop interfering in Church appointments Gregory took drastic action: he excommunicated Henry IV. Henry was forced to beg for pardon, barefoot and dressed in simple woollen clothes. Peace was restored but not for long. Henry IV marched on Rome and Gregory was forced to flee. Henry appointed his own pope, Clement III, while Gregory continued to claim he was the true pope.

4. **Holy war.** Gregory set up his own military force called the Knights of St Peter who defended the papacy against secular rulers. The pope developed the idea of holy war. This was a war which God supported and which brought spiritual benefits to those who participated. In 1074, Gregory VII even offered to lead an army against the Seljuk Turks himself. His conflict with Henry IV prevented it, but it was a sign of things to come.

3. **Reduced violence in Europe.** Gregory tried to restrain the nobles and knights of Latin Christendom from violent attacks on each other. He tried to channel their aggression by encouraging them to fight external enemies rather than other Christians. The pope encouraged French and Spanish nobles to fight against Muslims in Spain. He also promised the Normans that their sins would be forgiven for fighting against the Muslims in Sicily.

▲ Pope Gregory VII, from a twelfth-century manuscript

Where do the origins of the First Crusade lie?

Urban II

Urban was in his fifties when he became pope in 1088. He had been born into a noble family in northern France and had attended the cathedral school at Rheims. He followed a career in the Church, and in his mid-thirties Urban made the difficult decision to become a monk. His work at the great reforming monastery of Cluny encouraged him to improve the condition of the Church in Latin Christendom.

In 1088, the papacy was still weak and vulnerable. Pope Gregory VII had alienated many people in the Church through his radical reforms. Urban knew that he had to tread more carefully, but he also knew that he had to strengthen the power of the papacy if the Latin Church was to be further reformed. In the policies Urban pursued after 1088, it is not difficult to find some of the origins of the First Crusade:

1. Urban was well aware of the tension between the Latin Church and the Byzantine Church in the east. He was determined to heal the great split between the two Churches that had occurred in 1054. Urban sent messages of goodwill to Alexios I and tensions eased. Without this, the 1095 appeal for help from Alexios which sparked the First Crusade may never have happened.
2. Urban continued Gregory VII's policy of supporting the Christian reconquest of Spain and Sicily. He told Christian nobles and knights who fought the Muslims in al-Andalus that their military work was an act of penitence. He also offered spiritual rewards to the Normans of southern Italy who were driving the Muslims from Sicily. The First Crusade which Urban II triggered in 1095 was not the first holy war against Islam.

By 1095, the recovery of the papacy had begun, but Urban knew that there was still some way to go if he was to achieve his ambition of becoming the powerful spiritual leader of a reformed Latin Church. The appeal from Alexios I gave him an opportunity to start a holy war that could fulfill this ambition.

> ## Reflect
> How could you argue that the origins of the First Crusade lie in the ambitions of Urban II?

▲ Pope Urban II, from a fourteenth-century manuscript

Review

1. Highlight the labels on your three annotated maps to show which places and developments provide the strongest evidence for the origins of the First Crusade.
2. Discuss your ideas with a partner. How far do you agree about the origins of the First Crusade?
3. Write an essay to explain whether you agree with the following statement: '**The origins of the First Crusade lie in the weaknesses of Latin Christendom in the late eleventh century.**'

CLOSER LOOK 1

Finding out about the First Crusade

A wide range of sources can help us to find out about the First Crusade:

- We can still follow some of the ancient routes which the crusaders followed on their way to Jerusalem.
- Traces still remain of some of the town walls, castles, mosques and churches which the crusaders encountered.
- In archives and libraries, we can still find fascinating written documents such as letters, legal documents, songs, sermons and accounts that all help to shed light on the story of the First Crusade.

One of the richest sources that historians use to study the First Crusade are chronicles. Several of these chronicles were written at the end of the eleventh century or soon afterwards. The story of the First Crusade was so remarkable that different versions continued to be produced throughout the medieval period and beyond.

One of the earliest chronicles of the First Crusade, the *Historia*, was written by William of Tyre in 1184. On the left is a page from a thirteenth-century French translation of William of Tyre's chronicle. As you can see, the pages from some medieval chronicles even included small images of imagined scenes from the First Crusade.

The text and images from chronicle accounts give fascinating glimpses into all sorts of details about the First Crusade, from personalities and rivalries between crusader princes to detailed accounts of the day-to-day hardships that the crusading forces and their Muslim counterparts endured.

◀ A page from a thirteenth-century translation of William of Tyre's *Historia*, originally written in 1184

24

Finding out about the First Crusade

Chronicles

Chronicles often contain fascinating details that help us to understand the world of the First Crusade. However, historians have to be careful when using the accounts of chroniclers:

- Some of the chroniclers took part in the First Crusade and their writing was based on their own experience. Others based their account on what they had read or been told. None of the chronicles were written during the First Crusade itself.
- Chroniclers did not see themselves as historians: they were not trying to give a full and balanced account. Instead, they were writing from their own perspective, or that of their patron.
- Most chroniclers were monks from Europe. Their accounts were written from a Latin Christian perspective so do not always give historians the full picture.

Below you can find out about four chronicles that have been widely used by historians.

> **Reflect**
>
> For each chronicle, consider:
> 1. How could the chronicle be useful for a historian studying the First Crusade?
> 2. Why would a historian need to be careful when using the chronicle?

A History of the Expedition to Jerusalem, 1095–1127 by Fulcher of Chartres

Fulcher was educated at the great cathedral school of Chartres in northern France. He was part of the group of crusaders who left France with Stephen of Blois and Robert of Normandy in 1096. At Antioch he became chaplain to Baldwin of Boulogne and travelled with him to Edessa. Because of this he did not take part in the siege of Jerusalem. When Baldwin became the ruler of Jerusalem in December 1099, Fulcher continued as his chaplain. He wrote his chronicle in Jerusalem between 1100 and 1128. At the time of writing, he might have been trying to attract Europeans to come and settle in the Holy Land.

Gesta Francorum

The author of the *Gesta Francorum* ('The Deeds of the Franks') is unknown, but it is likely that he was a Norman or Italian knight. Historians think that this chronicle was probably written between 1101 and 1103. This makes it one of the earliest complete accounts of the First Crusade. As a result, it was much copied by others. The *Gesta* gives an account of the First Crusade from November 1095 to August 1099. Overall, it is written in a measured style, but there are passages which seem to give exaggerated accounts of particular events. Up until Antioch the author's perspective seems to support Bohemond. After Antioch it is more supportive of Raymond of Toulouse. Like many other chroniclers, the author of the *Gesta Francorum* disliked the Byzantines.

The Alexiad by Anna Komnena

Anna was the daughter of Alexios I. She favoured her father and disliked his successors. When Anna tried to overthrow one of her father's successors, she was sent to a convent where, isolated and resentful, she lived without access to her father's friends for 30 years. *The Alexiad* is a history of her father's reign. It had been started by her husband and Anna decided to complete it, probably around the year 1146. It describes her father's wars against the Seljuks and the Normans with vivid descriptions of battles. Anna was not an eyewitness, but had met crusader leaders in Constantinople when she was fourteen. She spoke to her relatives and used the Byzantine archives to write *The Alexiad*.

History of the Franks who captured Jerusalem by Raymond of Aguilers

Before the First Crusade, Raymond of Aguilers was canon to Adhemar of Le Puy (the papal legate for the First Crusade) in France. He accompanied Bishop Adhemar and Raymond of Toulouse, eventually becoming Raymond's chaplain. His chronicle is written from a southern French point of view, and is usually very positive about Raymond. Some historians think he might have started writing while actually on crusade, maybe at Antioch, although he did not complete his full account until 1100. In his chronicle he makes many references to the Bible and writes in great detail about the spiritual experiences of the crusaders.

2 Responses

What was so remarkable about the start of the First Crusade?

In November 1095, Pope Urban stood in a field at the edge of the French town of Clermont. There was a chill in the mountain air as he began to speak. This was a message that he could not deliver in the great cathedral church of Clermont, where he had spent the past ten days meeting with hundreds of bishops and abbots. No building in the French town could hold the crowd that had gathered to hear him preach.

Urban had let it be known in advance that this would be no ordinary sermon. The moment had arrived when he would make public the appeal for help that the Emperor Alexios had sent in March of that year. Pope Urban was about to call on Christians in the west to help their brothers and sisters in the east. This call has become known as the 'preaching' of the First Crusade.

▶ A nineteenth-century engraving showing Pope Urban II preaching the First Crusade at Clermont in 1095. From Cassell's *Illustrated History of England*, 1865

Reflect

How does this nineteenth-century illustration try to show:

- the importance of the pope
- the interest in his message?

What was so remarkable about the start of the First Crusade?

Chroniclers reported that Pope Urban's audience was electrified as he described in terrifying detail the advance of the Muslim Seljuk Turks into Christian lands in the eastern Mediterranean. The chronicler Fulcher of Chartres described the effect of Urban's words as he called upon Christians in western Europe to go to the aid of the Byzantine Emperor Alexios:

> After these words were spoken and the audience inspired to enthusiasm, many of them, thinking that nothing could be more worthy, at once promised to go and to urge earnestly those who were not present to do likewise.

Urban's call to arms spread with astonishing speed across Europe. Its impact was enormous and it created great excitement. When Alexios had first appealed to Urban for help he seems to have expected that the pope might send him a few hundred armed knights. Instead Alexios received wave after wave of fervent western Christians who saw themselves as soldiers of Christ. In 1103, the writer of *Gesta Francorum* described how

> through all the regions and countries of Gaul, the Franks, upon hearing such reports [of Urban's sermon], caused crosses to be sewed on their right shoulders, saying that they followed with one accord the footsteps of Christ, by which they had been redeemed from the hand of hell.

Between 50,000 and 100,000 people 'took the cross', making a solemn vow to complete a 2000-mile pilgrimage to Jerusalem and waging war on the people they saw as God's enemies.

The Enquiry

The start of the First Crusade was remarkable: something new and dramatic was happening in the hearts and minds of many Christians in western Europe. In the year or so following Pope Urban's sermon at Clermont, the shock waves spread rapidly across Europe and into Asia. The events of those months have continued to fascinate and alarm people for over nine centuries.

In this enquiry you will focus on the period between November 1095, when Pope Urban started to preach the crusade, to December 1096, by which time the first crusaders were engaged in bloody battle with Muslims in the east.

Your challenge is to identify and explain what was so remarkable about the start of the First Crusade. You will do this by making three spider diagrams. These will focus on **what was so remarkable about**:

- **Pope Urban's call to crusade**
- **The responses of the Latin Christians**
- **The so-called 'People's Crusade'**

Your first diagram might be structured like this:

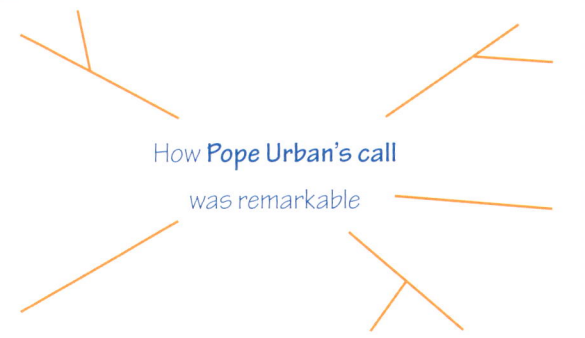

You can use as many lines as you wish with extra ones branching out to give further details. Be sure to identify and explain as many 'remarkable' features as you can and arrange them on your diagram.

In each section, watch out for the adjectives we use to describe events. They may be your best hints about what was so 'remarkable' about the start of this crusade.

Pope Urban's call to crusade

In itself, Alexios's appeal to the pope for aid against the Seljuk Turks was nothing particularly extraordinary. Byzantine emperors had made similar appeals in the past but Urban exploited the situation with exceptional energy and skill. He believed that it could help him further strengthen the power of the papacy and deepen people's Christian faith.

> **Record**
>
> As you read pages 28–31, make your first spider diagram, as explained on page 27. Watch out for signs of anything new, unusual or particularly powerful taking place.

Urban's sermon at Clermont

Unfortunately, the only records we have of what Urban actually said in his sermon come from sources that were written from memory, sometimes many years afterwards. Unsurprisingly, these sources often say quite different things. This means that historians have to be very careful about taking these different versions at face value. They compare the accounts and study them alongside Urban's letters and official documents from that time. From this research they have established what the original sermon probably said and why it had such an enormous impact on those who were there to hear it.

One of the most important accounts of Urban's sermon comes from the chronicle of Fulcher of Chartres. He wrote this around 1100. Eyewitnesses recalled this very special sermon for years afterwards and Fulcher may be basing his account on their memories.

▼ A statue of Pope Urban II that stands in the French village where Urban was born. It was erected in 1887

> There [is] an urgent task which belongs to both you and God: you must hasten to carry aid to your brothers living in the east, who need your help for which they have so often pleaded.
>
> The Turks have attacked the Christians in the east as many of you already know. They have seized more and more of the Christians' lands, have defeated them in seven battles, killed or captured many people, have destroyed churches, and have devastated the kingdom of God. If you allow them to continue much longer they will conquer God's faithful people much more extensively.
>
> Therefore with earnest prayer I, or not I, but God exhorts you as Christians to keep urging men of all ranks, knights as well as foot-soldiers, rich and poor, to hasten to exterminate this vile race from our lands and to aid the Christian people in time. I address those present; I proclaim it to those absent; moreover Christ commands it. For all those going, there will be forgiveness of sins if they die while marching by land, or crossing by sea or in fighting the pagans. This I grant to all who go, through the power given to me by God.

Other chroniclers describe how the crowds responded with enormous enthusiasm and Latin chants of 'Deus vult!' meaning 'God wills it!'

> **Reflect**
>
> What can Fulcher's report of Urban's sermon tell us about:
> - the situation facing Christians in the east
> - Urban's opinion of the Seljuk Turks
> - why Christians might have wanted to join the crusade?

What was so remarkable about the start of the First Crusade?

Urban's careful preparation

The positive response to Urban's sermon at Clermont was partly due to his ability as a preacher, but it was also due to his skills as an organiser. The preparation had started months before, in March 1095, when representatives from the Emperor Alexios came to Urban asking for help against the Seljuk Turks. Urban received them at a meeting of Church leaders where he was again looking for ways to re-assert the strength of the papacy.

Alexios's plea for help against the Turks gave Urban another chance to assert his authority. He could use this opportunity to re-unite the Christians of the west (Roman Catholics) with the Greek-speaking Christians of the Byzantine Empire. But he needed to be sure of a really good response when he called on western Christians to help their brothers and sisters in the east. That is why he left little to chance and spent the spring carefully preparing what he should say, and when and where he should say it. He came from a noble family in France and had strong support among leading families and churches there. This made it the perfect place to launch what became the First Crusade.

▲ Pope Urban's tour of France, July 1095–July 1096

Urban's tour of France, July to November 1095

In July 1095, Urban rode from Italy into France. The arrival of the pope with his train of followers stretching for miles behind him must have made a huge impression on local people. Although Urban was heading for Clermont, he first travelled around a wide area in the south-east of France and northwards to the great abbey of Cluny where he had worked for many years. Local people were delighted: here was the pope himself before their eyes – and he was a Frenchman too!

This exhausting and very unusual public journey won Urban support from Church leaders and influential families. He stayed for a while with Adhemar, the Bishop of Le Puy, and with Raymond, Count of Toulouse, the greatest lord of southern France. Urban exploited this opportunity to influence them and they both went on to become important leaders of the crusade. It all laid the foundations for the very positive response when he preached the crusade weeks later at Clermont. In fact, Bishop Adhemar was the very first person to respond, becoming the first crusader.

Urban's tour of France, December 1095 to July 1096

Urban did not rest after preaching at Clermont. He spent the next eight months travelling around western and southern France. On his 2000-mile journey he used every method known to the medieval world to persuade people to join the crusade. He preached the crusade at Limoges, Angers, Le Mans, Tours and Nîmes. He led grand parades and ceremonies, held discussions and wrote letters to abbeys, monasteries and local lords. The response was just as positive as it had been in Clermont. By August, he was back in northern Italy after leading a propaganda campaign greater and more successful than any the Catholic Church had ever seen.

> ## Reflect
> What was remarkable about Pope Urban's great preaching tour?

▶ Pope Urban on his great tour of France, from a fourteenth-century manuscript

29

Urban's vision

Urban's powerful preaching and his carefully organised tour launched the First Crusade, but it was his really powerful new blend of four existing ideas that gave the message its power. These are shown below.

The fear of purgatory

The western Church taught medieval Christians that the souls of really wicked people would go straight to hell. Most souls, however, would spend time in 'purgatory' where they would be 'purged' or cleansed. This cleansing involved a time of terrible suffering which would eventually make them pure enough to go to heaven.

Urban knew that his audience would be eager to find ways of shortening the time they might spend in purgatory – or avoiding it completely.

The importance of pilgrimage

Pilgrimages (journeys to a holy place) had been popular for hundreds of years. You learned on pages 8 and 16 how pilgrims would travel to sites near and far to pray at a shrine of a saint where his or her holy relics might bring miracles.

But pilgrimages could also serve as yet another form of penance that could reduce time spent in purgatory. The further a pilgrim travelled and the greater the hardship they endured on the way, the more effective the pilgrimage was as an act of penitence.

The idea of 'holy war'

Church leaders could declare a conflict to be a holy war if they thought that God wanted to use it to destroy his enemies.

In the decades before the crusade, holy wars had been fought against heathens (non-Christians) such as Vikings and Muslims in Spain and Sicily. Pope Gregory VII had planned to lead an expedition to defend Byzantium against the Turks in 1074, but decided that his position was too weak to make it happen. When Pope Urban used Norman knights to drive back the armies of the Holy Roman Emperor, he declared that it was a holy war.

The power of penance

As you read on page 21, the Roman Catholic Church believed in 'penance'. This taught that people could cut their time in purgatory by doing 'acts of penitence'.

These acts of penitence included:
- fasting (going without food or drink for long periods)
- saying prayers time and time again
- giving alms (money, food or property) to support the Church or to help needy people.

▲ A medieval sword

Urban's promise

In some holy wars before 1095, popes had made vague promises of spiritual rewards to people who took part. They told Christians who fought against Muslims in Spain, for example, that it would count as much as any pilgrimage as a way of paying for past sins.

Pope Urban took this much further: he promised that any Christian who travelled east to fight Muslims would be granted a full pardon for all their sins and would never have to do any other penance again. They would spend no time at all in purgatory but pass straight to heaven when they died. Urban was offering a completely new way of gaining forgiveness of sins. This was an astonishing promise that must have thrilled his hearers.

Reflect

1. Which of the four ideas above can you detect in the extract from Fulcher of Chartres on page 28?
2. What was so new about the promise made by Pope Urban in 1095?

What was so remarkable about the start of the First Crusade?

The appeal of Jerusalem

You may have noticed that in the extract by Fulcher of Chartres on page 28, Pope Urban never mentioned Jerusalem. He simply urges Christians to travel to the lands that Turks had taken from the Byzantine Christian Empire in the east. That would fit with the request that had reached him from Alexios. But in other accounts of the sermon at Clermont, Urban does refer very directly to Jerusalem. This has caused historians to disagree about how serious Urban was in his goal of liberating Jerusalem.

- Historians such as H.E. Mayer have argued that Urban was not that serious about freeing Jerusalem. It was only when other people started talking about it that he began to mention it in his letters.
- Other historians such as Jonathan Riley-Smith argue instead that freeing Jerusalem was always an important goal for Urban, especially as for Christians in western Europe it was the holiest place on earth.

Even if he only introduced the idea after his sermon at Clermont, Urban definitely did write letters calling on western Christians to capture Jerusalem and liberate Christians in the Holy Land from living under Muslim rule. It is clear that this appeal to liberate Jerusalem was hugely influential in persuading people to join the crusade. Jerusalem was the most holy pilgrimage destination. Pilgrims from western Europe had been travelling there for hundreds of years. It was where Christ had died and, according to Christian beliefs, had risen from the dead.

Some years later, around 1122, the chronicler Robert the Monk captured the sense of outrage that stirred in Latin Christians when they were reminded that this most holy city was being ruled by Muslim masters:

> Jerusalem is the navel of the world … The redeemer of the race [Jesus Christ] illuminated this land by his coming, graced it with his living there, made it holy by his suffering, redeemed it by his death, distinguished it by his burial. This royal city, set in the centre of the world, is now held captive by its enemies and is enslaved … by people who do not know God.

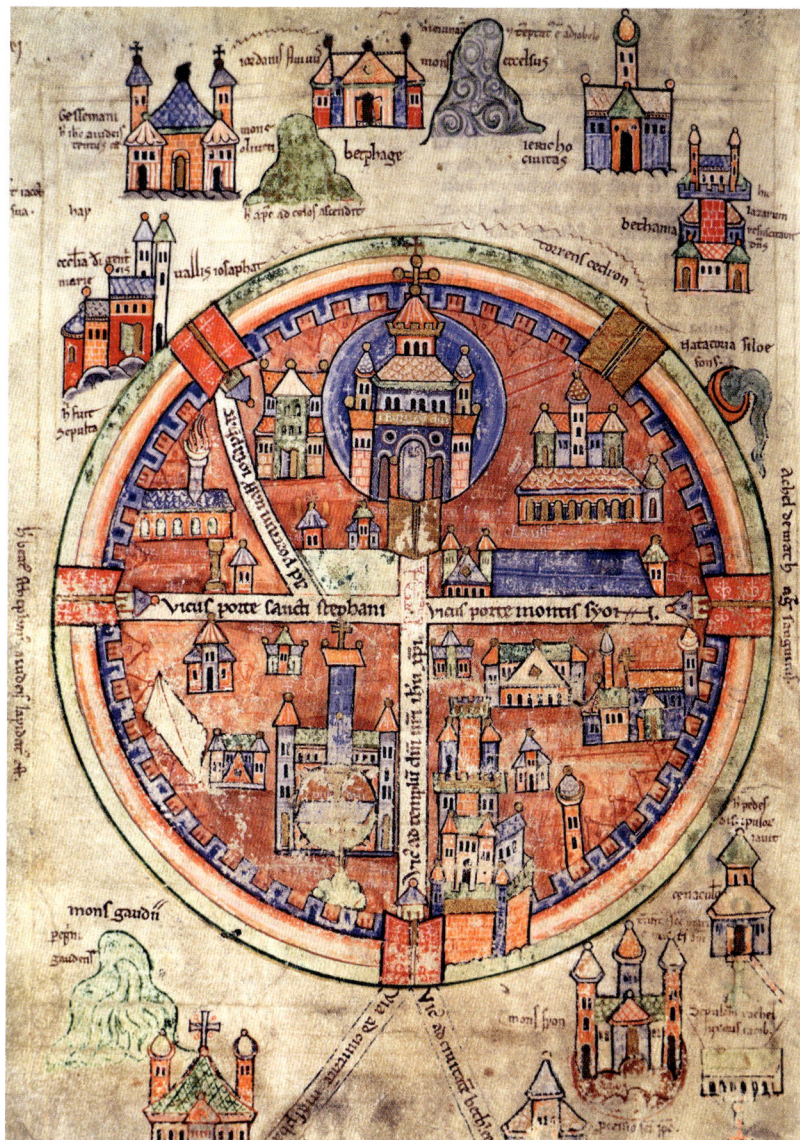

▲ A map showing Jerusalem and its surrounding area. From a thirteenth-century French manuscript. Notice how the Christian artist has made the streets form a cross at the heart of the city

Reflect

Some historians call the First Crusade an 'armed pilgrimage' while others call it a 'holy war'. Which, if any, do you think is the better description, and why?

Record

By now you should have made your first spider diagram showing what was remarkable about Pope Urban's call to crusade.

Compare your diagram with some by your fellow-students. You may be able to help each other by adding new examples or improving the explanations you have given.

The responses of Latin Christians

> ## Record
> As you read pages 32–37, make your second spider diagram, as explained on page 27. In the centre, write 'How the **responses of Latin Christians** were remarkable'.
>
> Watch out, in particular, for anything about the number and different types of people who responded and how far this matched what Pope Urban and Alexios had expected to see.

Look closely at this statue. The man wears a travelling cloak and carries a staff and purse, the symbols of the pilgrim. You will see he also has a cross sewn on the front of his cloak, the symbol of the crusader. The woman has her arms wrapped around him, hinting at the heartache felt when a family member left to go crusading or their joy when he or she returned. At best, families like this faced a separation of many years. All crusaders knew it was very likely they would not return at all.

The diversity of the crusaders

Unsurprisingly, the vast majority of western Europeans chose not to go crusading, but in the months after Urban's sermon at Clermont between 50,000 and 100,000 Latin Christians from western Europe took the cross, from as far north as England and as far south as Sicily.

The crusaders spoke more than twenty different languages. Most were men of fighting age. But not all. Many were far from the skilled and experienced fighters Pope Urban had in mind. Vast numbers of peasants and townspeople joined the crusade, including thousands of women and children who went as non-combatants. In regions where a lord chose to join the crusade, or where church leaders supported the pope's Reform Movement, large groups of local people took the cross.

Priests and members of the religious orders, including at least one nun, also joined, despite Urban's efforts to stop them. One woman, who led her own religious sect, took her goose with her, believing that it was filled with the Holy Spirit (at least until it died).

So enormous was the response that, by autumn 1096, Urban was working to calm down the over-enthusiasm of some. He wrote the letter shown on the right to Christians in Bologna, in northern Italy, in September 1096.

▲ A statue of a crusader and his wife at Belval Priory, France, c.1150. This is Count Hugh de Vaudemont who fought in the Second Crusade in 1147

We have heard that some of you have formed the desire to go to Jerusalem, and you should know that this is pleasing to us. Those who go, not from the desire of the goods of this world but for the good of their souls and the liberty of the churches, will be relieved of the penance for all of their sins … because they have exposed themselves and their property to danger out of their love of God and their neighbour.

To neither clerics nor monks, however, do we give permission to go without the permission of their bishops or abbots. Let it be the bishops' duty to permit their parishioners to go only with the advice of the clergy. Nor should young married men rashly set out on the journey without the agreement of their wives.

> ## Reflect
> What can Urban's letter tell us about who wanted to join the crusade and why they might want to go?

What was so remarkable about the start of the First Crusade?

Feudal society

The society of Urban's day, especially in France, was organised as a hierarchy, sometimes known as the feudal system. This bound people together through a system of rewards and duties. The diagram below gives a very simple outline of how the hierarchy worked.

> ### Reflect
> 1. Which of the groups below would Urban particularly want to join the crusade?
> 2. What clues can you find to explain why people from all levels of society (except kings) joined the crusade?

At the head of eleventh-century society were **kings**. They had considerable power and wealth but they had to take care not to lose their lands and even their crowns to ambitious dukes and other nobles. No kings joined the crusade – they did not dare to leave their kingdoms.

▲ King Philip I of France, carved c.1108

Just below the kings were the **dukes and other nobles, sometimes known as 'princes'**. Some controlled territories bigger than those of the king. In the eleventh century they were regularly involved in wars against each other as they tried to increase their land and power or to win the approval of the king. It was this sort of warlike behaviour that Urban II was keen to control.

▲ The Duke of Aquitaine removing the tongue of a rival lord, from a thirteenth-century manuscript

Below the 'princes' were **knights**. They received land from the nobles in return for providing military service whenever the lord required it. In France, the richest lived in castles that were dotted across the landscape. They would fight for their lord, wage bloody feuds with local rivals or plunder the countryside.

▲ An eleventh-century knight's castle in northern France

▲ Peasants from an eleventh-century manuscript

For **the vast majority of people**, life was hard. Most served a local lord or knight. Some might have worked as servants or cooks, but millions were peasants doing back-breaking work on the land. Most would spend their whole life within a few miles of home, unless their lord took them to serve him on a military campaign.

By the 1070s, life was particularly difficult for most peasants. As the population grew there was even less land to share out. Famines became a regular part of life and large numbers of landless peasants roamed the countryside, hoping to find some way to improve their life.

33

The leaders of the crusade: the great princes

The crusade was a highly unusual campaign because it did not have a single overall leader. Although Pope Urban launched the crusade, he did not lead it himself. Instead he appointed Bishop Adhemar of Le Puy as his representative and the crusade's spiritual leader.

The question of who would provide military leadership was more difficult. The most obvious choice would have been a king, but none joined. However a number of princes did. Four of these are described below. Princes like these brought with them large numbers of knights and other people from the regions they ruled.

> **Reflect**
>
> Historians disagree about whether the princes were more motivated by their religious beliefs or by 'material' concerns (the chance of gaining power, loot and land). Read the short biographies below and decide what motivated each man.

Raymond of Toulouse

Raymond was one of the richest and most powerful princes in western Christendom. He was in his mid-60s and had limited fighting experience. Famously he had lost an eye: some said fighting Muslims in Spain, others said because he had refused to pay Muslim taxes while on pilgrimage to Jerusalem.

Raymond had not always been a friend of the pope (he was excommunicated twice!), but by the 1080s was one of the leading members of the Church Reform Movement. The very day after Urban's sermon at Clermont, Raymond pledged his support. Raymond expected to be made leader of the crusade, along with his ally Bishop Adhemar of Le Puy, but Urban refused to confirm Raymond's leadership. It was another eight months before Raymond finally declared he would actually join the crusade.

Godfrey of Bouillon

Godfrey was in his mid-30s when he joined the crusade. He was the Duke of Lotharingia but his lands were not particularly profitable. Like Raymond of Toulouse, Godfrey was a second son, becoming a duke only when his uncle died. He had some experience of fighting but not of leading a war.

Godfrey was not known for being a friend of the Church. He had always been a strong supporter of the pope's enemy, Henry IV of Germany, and had a reputation for plundering Church lands if it suited his needs. He did, however, have a strong faith and was prepared to ignore past rivalries and answer the pope's call to crusade. He was joined on the crusade by his ambitious brother Baldwin, Count of Boulogne.

Bohemond of Taranto

Bohemond was one of the most gifted and experienced military leaders in western Europe. He was 40 years old when he joined the crusade. Although he was a Norman, he spent much of his life trying to take control of southern Italy and the island of Sicily. This meant fighting the Byzantine Empire, which also wanted to control the region.

His appearance struck fear and admiration into others. He was very tall and powerfully built. He took the cross in dramatic style by tearing his rich cloak into strips, which he and his supporters then sewed onto their own cloaks in the sign of the cross.

Bohemond was not rich. His father had made his younger brother his heir, leaving Bohemond virtually penniless and landless. When Bohemond joined the crusade, some said he hoped to restart a war against the Byzantines and to conquer for himself lands in the east.

Tancred

Tancred was the nephew of Bohemond and also lived in southern Italy. Tancred's biographer Ralph of Caen wrote:

> Frequently he burned with anxiety because the warfare he engaged in as a knight seemed to be against the Lord's [God's] commands. The Lord, in fact, ordered him to offer the cheek that had been struck together with his other cheek to the striker; but knighthood did not spare the blood of relatives … But after the judgement of Pope Urban granted forgiveness of all their sins to all Christians going out to fight the [Muslims], then at last, as if previously asleep, his vigour was aroused, his powers grew, his eyes opened, his courage was born. For before … his mind was divided, uncertain whether to follow in the footsteps of the Bible or the world.

▲ A carving of knights fighting each other on horseback. From an archway in a church in northern Italy, made c.1120

The warriors of the crusade: the knights

The knights were clearly the people that Urban and Alexios had in mind when they appealed for help. These were professional warriors, the most skilled, experienced and powerful soldiers in the west.

They were armed with swords and were protected in battle by chain mail, shields and helmets, but it was the horse that gave a knight his biggest advantage on the battlefield. Greatly helped by the invention of the stirrup, knights could sit firmly above their enemies swinging their swords or attacking with their spears held out before them, like those in the carving above. They led heavy cavalry charges on powerful warhorses specially bred and trained for battle. These were extremely expensive, costing five times more than an ox, which was the most valuable possession a peasant family might own.

Most knights inherited their wealth as land passed down from their fathers. During the eleventh century, as the population grew and good land became scarcer, the old custom of sharing out land into smaller and smaller parcels was being ended. Instead, it gave way to a new approach where only one son, usually the eldest, would inherit the land. Landless knights, including those from wealthier peasant families who could barely afford their horse and armour, might need to find a new line of work.

By 1095, if a young knight with no land or castle could not marry into a land-holding family or find work serving a lord as a professional soldier, he might enter the Church. Knights were as likely to have a religious faith as any other medieval person but the prospect of becoming a priest or monk did not appeal to men of action. To many men like this, Urban's call to crusade seemed to be an extraordinary, heaven-sent opportunity. Around 1108, the monk, Guibert of Nogent, explained in his chronicle that:

> God has begun in our time holy wars, so that the knights and the crowd running in their wake … might find a new way of gaining salvation. [Now] they are not forced to … choose the monastic life or any religious profession, as used to be the custom. Instead, they can attain some measure of God's grace while pursuing their own careers, with liberty and in the clothing to which they are accustomed.

Reflect

Why would some knights be especially pleased to learn that Pope Urban had called for a crusade in 1095?

Explaining the knights' motives

In France alone there were nearly 50,000 knights but historians have estimated that only about 7000 knights from all over Europe went on crusade. This raises the question of what made some go and what made so many others remain at home.

For many years, historians suggested that 'material' motives were most important in driving knights to join the crusade. According to this theory, sons who failed to inherit land (see page 35) went on the crusade hoping to gain land, treasure or money.

More recently, historians have challenged this interpretation. They argue that material motives were less important than spiritual ones. Much of their evidence comes from charters which earlier historians had rarely used when doing their research.

Charters

▲ A thirteenth-century crusader charter

A knight or his family would often have to make big sacrifices to join the crusade. It might cost him four or five times his annual income to buy the equipment he needed. He, like the great lords and princes, often had to sell or mortgage land to raise the money needed. He also had to arrange who would look after his lands at home in his absence. A written record of these legal agreements was often kept in documents called 'charters'. These provide some good evidence of where the crusading knights lived, how wealthy they were and even why they went.

Some charters reveal genuine religious commitment, even in knights whose previous life may have been far from holy. In one case, a knight called Bertrand of Moncontour wanted to join the crusade but was plagued by guilt. Bertrand's dying father had granted some land to an abbey but Bertrand kept it for himself. This extract from a charter made in 1098 shows what he did:

> Bertrand of Moncontour desires to go to Jerusalem but believes that the journey of God [the crusade] will be of no use to him while he still possesses the land that he stole. He therefore confesses his guilt and restores to the monks of that abbey all that he took from them.

Historians have to consider all the evidence that is available if they want to explain the knights' motives for joining the crusade. This box shows some more findings from historians' research:

- Some knights had clauses added into their charters that covered the possibility that they might settle in the east.
- Charters usually emphasised the knight's spiritual motives, often mentioning a desire to free Jerusalem. But most knights could not read or write and their charters were mostly written for them by monks or priests who may have added their own view of the crusade to the document.
- From the very start, Urban seems to have been worried that people might join the crusade for the wrong reasons. The decree of the Council of Clermont granted the remission of penance to those who crusaded 'for devotion only, not to gain honour or money'.
- Pope Urban promised crusaders they could enjoy 'undisturbed possession' of the lands they conquered.
- Most crusaders returned home to Europe after Jerusalem was taken. By 1100, just 300 western knights remained in the lands conquered by the crusade.
- We now know that most crusaders returned home poorer than they set out.

Here is what historian Thomas Asbridge wrote about this debate in his 2010 book, *The Crusades*:

> The once fashionable myth that crusaders were self-serving, disinherited, land-hungry younger sons must be discarded. Crusading was instead an activity that could bring spiritual and material rewards, but it was in the first instance both an intimidating and extremely costly activity. Devotion inspired Europe to crusade.

Reflect

How useful are the extract from Bertrand's charter, the list of historians' findings and the interpretation of Thomas Asbridge for a historian studying the motives of crusader knights?

What was so remarkable about the start of the First Crusade?

The mass of the crusade: the peasants and others

There was a 'cascade' effect when a lord or knight chose to join the crusade. Princes arranged for foot soldiers, archers and crossbowmen to march with them. They also took carpenters and blacksmiths to make and mend equipment and merchants who were supposed to keep the armies supplied. Knights took spare horses, horseshoes, armour and weapons, leather for tack and saddles, clothing, hunting birds and dogs, tents, saddlebags, sacks, barrels and pack animals to carry all this equipment. This meant that they also took farriers, huntsmen, squires and chaplains (priests) to look after their daily needs.

Other crusaders were not part of a knight's or prince's household. They were peasants or townspeople with little or no fighting experience. Some travelled with their wives and children and even older relatives. Many of these people had barely travelled beyond their village or town before.

▼ A crowd from an eleventh-century French manuscript. People such as these made up the mass of crusaders

The motives of the masses

Unlike the knights and princes, there are few sources of evidence about the motives of ordinary people. They did not write charters, as they had no land to mortgage or sell to raise money, and could not read or write. Around 1110, a German monk called Ekkehard explained why so many were prepared to risk everything and join the crusade:

> The western Franks could easily be persuaded to leave their farms. For they had been severely afflicted for some years by civil wars, hunger and death … Some said that they were summoned to the Promised Land by certain prophets newly arisen among them and by signs in the heavens and by revelations. Others recognised that they had been impelled to take such vows [to crusade] by all kinds of hardships. Certainly very many of them travelled weighed down by wives, children and all their domestic goods.

Reflect

1. What reasons does Ekkehard give to explain why ordinary people joined the First Crusade?
2. Why do you think whole families, young and old, joined the crusade together?

Historians know that life had been particularly hard in western Europe, especially in France, in the years leading up to the crusade. The population had risen sharply and this put more pressure on land and food supplies, especially as drought ruined several harvests in the 1090s. There had also been outbreaks of a gruesome disease called 'ergotism'. This was caused by eating bread made from mouldy rye. But the desire to escape hardship cannot have been their only motive: chronicles describe how these poorer crusaders wore the sign of the cross on their clothing and sang hymns as they made their way east.

Record

Complete your second spider diagram showing what was remarkable about the responses of Latin Christians to the call to crusade. Once again, you may want to share ideas with others.

The People's Crusade

Urban wanted an orderly and disciplined crusade. He announced that the princes would depart with their different groups on 15 August 1096. That date was chosen because at harvest time supplies would be more plentiful. It would also give the Byzantines plenty of time to prepare the routes that the crusaders were expected to follow to reach Constantinople.

But Urban and Alexios's careful planning could not control the enthusiasm they had unleashed. Popular preachers, unauthorised by the pope, travelled around Europe calling the urban and rural poor to crusade. Their fiery sermons stirred thousands to take the cross. The intense fervour of those who responded proved to be a real problem for both Urban and Alexios.

In early 1096, months earlier than Urban had intended and without his blessing, up to 30,000 people in different bands left their homes and set off for Jerusalem. This first, unofficial wave became known as the People's Crusade. Writing c.1130, the chronicler Albert of Aachen said that it included

> as many sinful as pious men: adulterers, murderers, thieves, perjurers and robbers; that is to say every sort of people of Christian faith, indeed even the female sex.

> **Record**
>
> As you read pages 38–41, make your final spider diagram, as explained on page 27. At the centre, write 'How **the People's Crusade** was remarkable'.
>
> In this section you learn about some deeply alarming incidents that caused shock and shame at the time of the First Crusade.

Leadership

The most famous leader of the People's Crusade was Peter the Hermit, who preached the crusade across central and northern France and the Rhineland. Some chronicles even suggest that his preaching stirred Urban II to action. Peter dressed like a beggar and was 'small in stature'. He had an extraordinary effect on his audience. In 1108, the chronicler Guibert of Nogent described Peter's impact:

> We saw him wander through cities and towns, spreading his teaching, surrounded by so many people, given so many gifts and acclaimed for such great piety, that I don't ever remember anyone equally honoured … whatever he did or said seemed like something divine. Even the hairs of his mule were torn out as though they were relics.

Peter and other popular preachers made no preparations for the journey to Jerusalem. Instead, the small bands set out on their own, terribly ill-equipped for the long journey ahead. Some sources suggest that Peter the Hermit's group had a wagon full of treasure, but if they did this was unusual. Most travelled with few supplies and little money to buy them. They had no pack animals and most had to walk the entire way.

Recent research by historians has challenged the view that the People's Crusade was completely chaotic. Educated priests, experienced knights and minor nobles took charge of some elements. The most well-known were the knight Walter Sans-Avoir from northern France and the German Count Emich of Leiningen from northern Germany.

▲ Peter the Hermit leading the People's Crusade, from a thirteenth-century French manuscript

> **Reflect**
>
> From the evidence on this page, what would you expect to be the greatest strengths and weaknesses of the People's Crusade?

Brutality against the Jews

In one of the most horrific episodes of the Middle Ages, the first victims of the People's Crusade were not Muslim Seljuk Turks but European Jews.

The first crusaders to travel through the Rhineland were led by Walter Sans-Avoir and Peter the Hermit. They forced Jewish communities to give them money but otherwise were fairly orderly. The violence broke out when another group, led by the ruthless German lord, Count Emich, followed them. Local people joined in as the crusaders forcibly converted Jews or murdered them and looted their property. As the summary below shows, the murders continued across the Rhineland for over a month. These attacks on Jews were called 'pogroms'. By the time the crusaders finally left the area, their pogroms had killed over 1500 Jews.

The massacres in the Rhineland – summer 1096

1. **Speyer, 3 May:** Twelve Jews who refused to convert were killed. The local bishop saved the rest.
2. **Worms, 18 May:** 500 Jews were killed despite being under the bishop's special protection.
3. **Mainz, 26 May:** After anti-Jewish riots inside the city, 1000 Jews were killed (see below).
4. **Cologne, 30 May:** Most Jews were hidden by Christian neighbours. The archbishop limited the violence but the synagogue was burned and several Jews who refused to convert were murdered.
5. **Metz, early June:** 22 Jews were killed. The crusaders then scattered. Some went home while others continued on their journey to Jerusalem.

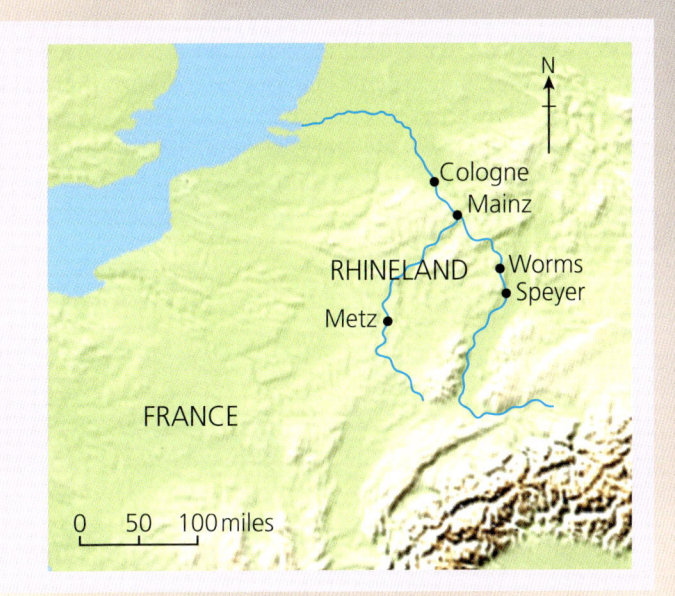

Mainz – the worst of the massacres

In May 1096, the large Jewish community in Mainz heard warnings from nearby towns that crusaders were burning synagogues, looting, stealing and killing as they tried to force Jews to convert. One of the leading culprits was Count Emich.

As Emich's crusaders approached Mainz, Jewish leaders went to the Christian archbishop pleading for protection. In return for 400 pieces of silver, the archbishop let them shelter in his palace and shut the city gates. But it was not enough. When Emich arrived outside the city walls, some sympathetic townspeople opened the gates. Crusaders poured into the city. The archbishop and his men fled, abandoning the Jews to their fate.

Some Jews tried to flee, tossing money from windows in an attempt to distract the crusaders. Others armed themselves, but they were quickly overwhelmed. The crusaders broke down the doors and slaughtered everyone they could find: men, women and children. Realising there was no way out, the remaining Jews made a desperate decision: taking knives they killed one another, preferring to die by their own hands.

Reasons for the attacks against the Jews

Anti-Semitism already had a long history in western Europe but it had never before led to such terrible violence. These events astonished and horrified many people at the time and the shocking violence of the People's Crusade threatened to destroy Urban's crusade before it had even left Europe.

Historians have suggested three main reasons that together may explain why anti-Semitic prejudice turned to brutal murder in 1096:

1. In their religious fervour, the crusaders failed to distinguish between Muslims and Jews. To their minds, both were enemies of Christianity.
2. Crusade preaching focused on freeing Jerusalem where Jesus had been crucified over a thousand years earlier. Christians had long blamed the Jews for this and these highly charged and poorly disciplined crusaders wanted revenge.
3. The crusaders were targeting wealthy Jews so they could buy supplies for their journey.

The journey to Constantinople

Through the summer of 1096, the various bands of the People's Crusade pushed eastwards towards Constantinople. They had ignored Pope Urban's plan and had set off before the harvest and without giving the Byzantines time to prepare supplies for them. Their intense desire to reach the Holy Land and their total confidence that God would protect them and give them victory were to be their undoing.

It is very hard to know precise numbers but historians believe that, by mid-August 1096, over half of all those who had joined the People's Crusade lay dead, mostly killed in battles against fellow Christians.

Walter Sans-Avoir
Walter Sans-Avoir and his crusaders left the Rhineland in mid-April 1096. In May, they crossed Hungary even though the king had not been expecting any crusaders until the autumn. He provided an armed escort to stop them scavenging crops, and so did Alexios when they reached the Byzantine Empire. Despite some trouble between a few crusaders and the armies of Alexios, Walter's group reached Constantinople on 1 August 1096.

▲ Routes taken by the different bands of the People's Crusade

Peter the Hermit
Peter the Hermit's larger force followed about a week after Walter, taking the same route. In Hungary and in the Byzantine Empire there were serious incidents. The crusaders resented the way they were being stopped from searching the countryside for supplies and fought with the forces that had been sent to escort them. In the last of these, at Nish on 3 July, Peter lost almost a quarter of his crusaders in a battle with the soldiers of Alexios. The rest of his group was allowed to press on and reached Constantinople on 15 August.

Volkmar, Gottshalk and Count Emich
The last groups of the People's Crusade left western Europe under these three men. All three led anti-Semitic pogroms, first in southern Germany, then in Prague and finally, under Count Emich, in Mainz (see page 39). Their ill-discipline and violence led to their downfall: all three armies were completely crushed on battlefields in Hungary after resisting the Hungarian king's armed escorts.

> **Reflect**
> Why did so few of those who joined the People's Crusade reach Constantinople?

More disaster at Constantinople
The Emperor Alexios had heard all about the ill-discipline of the forces of Walter Sans-Avoir and Peter the Hermit as they travelled through his lands. When they arrived at Constantinople in August 1096, it was worse than he had expected. Peter and Walter could not stop the crusaders from attacking palaces and stealing lead from church roofs. Their brutality, greed and unreliability fitted exactly the view that Greek Christians held of western Christians as crude and violent barbarians. The shocking behaviour of the so-called 'army of God' was bringing shame on Urban's grand plan.

What was so remarkable about the start of the First Crusade?

The final destruction of the People's Crusade

To protect his city, Alexios quickly forced the People's Crusade to cross the Bosphorus, the narrow strip of water separating Constantinople from Asia Minor. Once they had crossed they were supposed to stay in a base that had been set aside for them at Kibotos on the coast. Alexios expected them to wait there until the official crusade arrived. Messengers from the pope had assured him that the forces led by the princes should reach Constantinople within three months.

Annihilation, October 1096

In September 1096, however, the People's Crusade once again fell victim to ill-discipline and over-enthusiasm. While Peter the Hermit was in Constantinople organising supplies for the crusader camp, rival groups of French and German crusaders set off to attack Muslim-held towns, some of which were only about 25 miles away.

As they travelled along the Asian coast, fuelled by religious fervour and ignorant of local languages and people, the crusaders attacked Muslims and Christians alike. Some captured a Muslim castle but were soon besieged inside it by a large force of Turks. With no access to the well, which lay far beyond the castle's walls, the crusaders quickly ran out of water. Celebration turned to fear, then despair. After eight long days they surrendered, but this did not save them. Some 6000 were massacred.

When news of their deaths reached the main camp at Kibotos, the remaining crusaders were enraged. A few urged caution, but were over-ruled by hotter heads. Twenty thousand crusaders, led by 500 knights, rode out to battle the Turks. But they rode into a trap. Just three miles away, the Turks lay in wait for them. On 21 October, in a narrow, steep-sided valley, 20,000 crusaders were killed. When a relief force arrived from Byzantium, just 3000 remained alive. They were taken back to Constantinople where Alexios had them disarmed and held in a camp outside the city. By then, the first bands of the official crusade were on the way.

▲ An illustration by nineteenth-century artist Gustav Doré showing later groups of crusaders coming across the remains of the People's Crusade near Kibotos

Record

Complete your final spider diagram showing what was remarkable about the People's Crusade. Once again, you may want to share ideas with others.

Review

Look again at all three of your spider diagrams. From all the examples you have found, choose the six that you think provide the best answer to the question: **'What was so remarkable about the start of the First Crusade?'** Discuss your selection with others and explain why you chose them.

CLOSER LOOK 2

Robert Curthose, a Norman knight

This is the tomb of Robert, Duke of Normandy, one of the princes who joined the First Crusade and who lived through the entire expedition. His nickname was 'Robert Curthose' which can be translated as 'Robert Short-socks'. This was a reference to the length of his legs rather than his leggings (which actually seem quite long in his tomb sculpture!)

This short-legged, powerful warrior joined the crusade in 1096 when he was the Duke of Normandy. For many years before then, he was a knight, one of the sons of a famous father. A closer look at his life gives a deeper sense of the values, ambitions and lifestyle of the wealthier crusaders.

▲ The tomb monument of Robert Curthose, Duke of Normandy. This was made at Gloucester Cathedral, c.1230 about a century after Robert died

The rebellious son

Robert was born around 1051 and was the oldest child of William Duke of Normandy and his wife Matilda. You will know Duke William better as William the Conqueror. Despite being William's oldest son, Robert never fully won the confidence of his father. In 1073, not long after William became King of England, Robert dared to suggest that he might be allowed to rule Normandy. His father rejected the idea outright. Robert responded by gathering around him a group of knights and leading an armed rebellion in Normandy, sometimes facing his father directly in battle.

After father and son were reconciled in 1080, Robert went to live with his uncle, Duke Robert of Flanders, who later joined him on the crusade. Over the next few years, Robert moved from Flanders to Germany and Italy, using his undoubted gifts as a warrior to plunder the countryside. He also had several illegitimate children in this period. He was no 'knight in shining armour'.

Robert Curthose, a Norman knight

The famous crusader

When King William died in 1087, he made his younger son, William Rufus, King of England and made Robert the Duke of Normandy. The dying king clearly believed that Robert was too weak-willed to be a king, even though he had clearly shown that he was a powerful warrior in battle. The next few years proved William right: Robert became involved in plots to take England from his brother William Rufus and he ran up large debts in Normandy.

When Pope Urban preached the First Crusade in 1095, it was Robert's spiritual advisers who suggested that he might take part. Maybe they thought it would be good for his soul! It was William Rufus who raised a very heavy tax on the people of England to fund Robert's crusading. Robert handed his lands in Normandy to William Rufus for three years in return for a sum of money that turned him from being a debt-ridden noble to one of the wealthier crusader princes. William Rufus must have been very happy for the people of England to pay the price of removing his troublesome brother for a few years – and possibly forever.

While on the crusade, Robert built up a reputation as a fine and popular warrior, although he once again showed that he was weak on strategy. He returned to Normandy in 1101.

The powerless captive

As Robert journeyed back to Europe, he learned that William Rufus had died and that his youngest brother had quickly taken the throne of England as Henry I. Robert spent the next five years trying to win the English crown that he felt should be his.

His time as a crusader does not seem to have changed his habits in these years. One chronicler tells how Robert once missed a special sermon by a famous preacher: he overslept having spent the night before getting drunk with court jesters and harlots.

Robert's attempts to become King of England failed dismally. He was captured and held prisoner for 28 years until he died in 1134. King Henry I famously told the wider world that because Robert had been such a fine crusader,

> I have not kept him in irons like a captured enemy, but have lodged him as a noble pilgrim in a royal castle.

▼ An eighteenth-century engraving of a stained-glass window at the Abbey of Saint-Denis near Paris. The window was destroyed in the French Revolution, c.1789. It showed Robert of Normandy piercing a Turkish soldier with his lance in battle

In France, soon after he died, his exploits as a crusader were honoured in a splendid stained-glass window at the Abbey of Saint-Denis near Paris. Sadly that no longer exists. All we have as a monument is the fine tomb sculpture made for him in Gloucester Cathedral about 100 years after his death.

Reflect

From what you have read of his life, what do you think made Robert of Normandy want to be a crusader?

3 Into the Muslim world

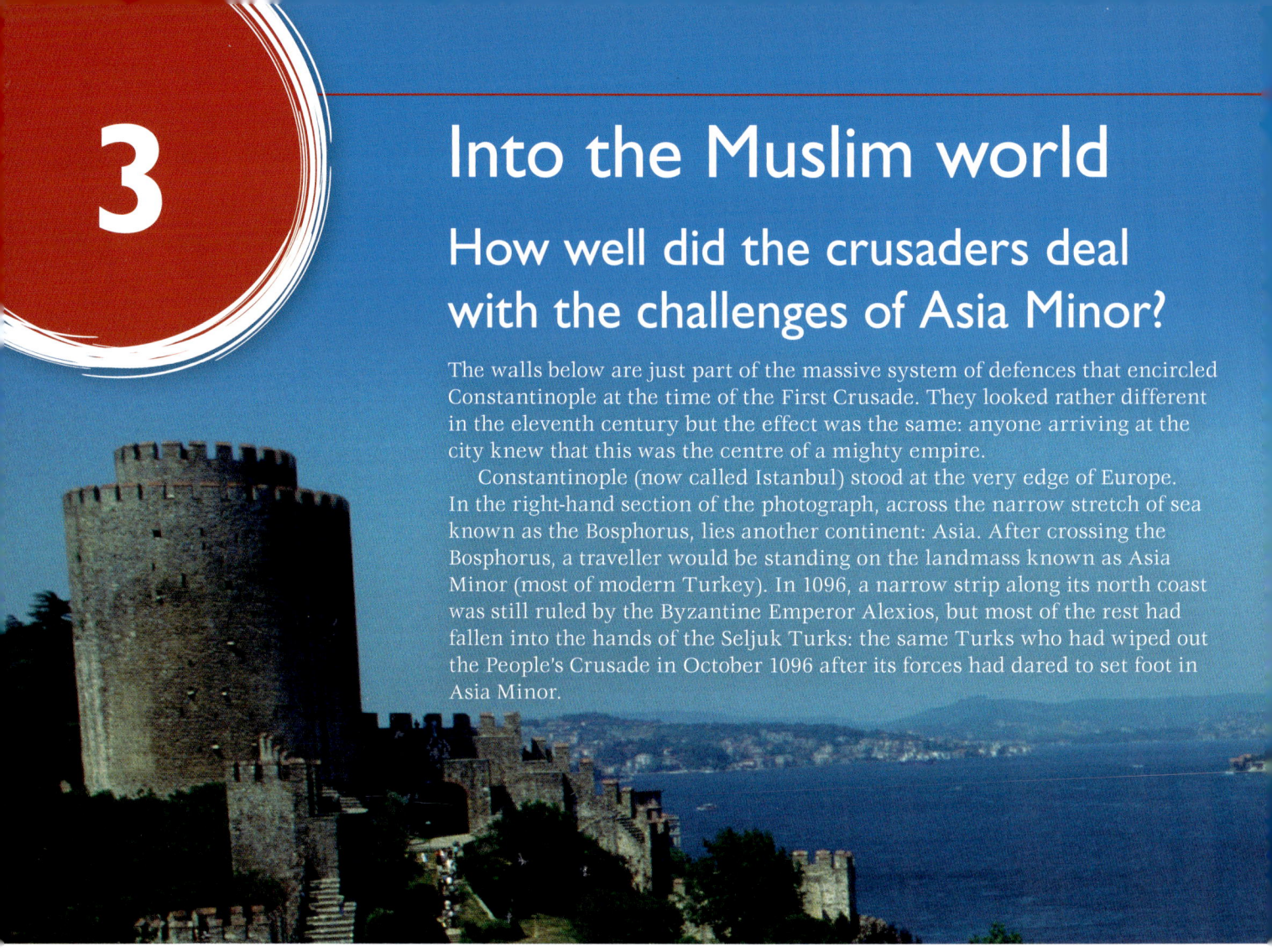

How well did the crusaders deal with the challenges of Asia Minor?

The walls below are just part of the massive system of defences that encircled Constantinople at the time of the First Crusade. They looked rather different in the eleventh century but the effect was the same: anyone arriving at the city knew that this was the centre of a mighty empire.

Constantinople (now called Istanbul) stood at the very edge of Europe. In the right-hand section of the photograph, across the narrow stretch of sea known as the Bosphorus, lies another continent: Asia. After crossing the Bosphorus, a traveller would be standing on the landmass known as Asia Minor (most of modern Turkey). In 1096, a narrow strip along its north coast was still ruled by the Byzantine Emperor Alexios, but most of the rest had fallen into the hands of the Seljuk Turks: the same Turks who had wiped out the People's Crusade in October 1096 after its forces had dared to set foot in Asia Minor.

▲ The view from the walls of Constantinople (Istanbul) over the Bosphorus to Asia Minor

The shocking destruction of the People's Crusade confirmed Alexios's worst fears. But even as he was establishing a camp for the survivors outside Constantinople in November 1096, the first of Pope Urban's official crusaders began to arrive in the city. Peter the Hermit, who was in Constantinople when the People's Crusade was crushed, joined this official crusade but no longer as a leader. This time the leaders were 'princes'.

Alexios was determined to make it clear who was really in charge. He sent officials and soldiers to meet each group of crusaders at the border. They escorted the crusaders to Constantinople. Messages between crusader groups were intercepted and read. But, as with the People's Crusade, even these careful preparations were not enough to stop crusaders fighting their Byzantine hosts, mostly over supplies.

There were some alarming and strange confrontations. On one occasion, the pope's representative Bishop Adhemar was thrown off his mule and beaten by Alexios's soldiers as they were trying to bring some troublesome crusaders under control. On another, the Byzantine fleet mistook ships carrying crusaders for pirates. This led to a serious skirmish in which a crusader crossbow bolt was fired straight through the shield and body armour of the Byzantine captain, lodging in his arm. A western priest was seen shooting arrows and hurling large stones and even barley cakes at the Byzantine sailors.

This was the same sort of misunderstanding and ill-feeling between eastern and western Christians that had ruined the People's Crusade. The official crusade seemed to be as ill-disciplined and incapable as the force led by Peter the Hermit. Another speedy crusading failure seemed likely.

Reflect

From what you have learned so far in this book, what sort of challenges do you think the crusaders could expect to face as they crossed into Asia Minor?

The Enquiry

When the first official crusaders arrived at the gates of Constantinople they had already travelled over 1500 miles, following similar routes to those shown on page 40. As they set up camp outside the city's walls, they learned of the terrible fate of the People's Crusade. They knew that their biggest challenges still lay ahead, beginning with Asia Minor.

In this enquiry you will learn about events between December 1096 and October 1097. These include:

1. negotiations between Alexios and the Crusade leaders
2. the crusaders' siege of Nicaea and their battle with the Turks at Dorylaeum
3. their journey across Asia Minor.

As you work you will be making 'challenge cards'.

a) Describe the challenge.
b) Explain why this was challenging.
c) Explain how well you think the crusaders coped with that challenge.

▲ Asia Minor and the Near East, c.1097

Negotiations: Alexios and the crusade leaders

Between October and December 1096, many thousands of western crusaders arrived at Constantinople. The Byzantines gave them the name of 'Franks' even though they came from many different regions, not just the area we now call France. Anna Komnena recalled their arrival in her *The Alexiad*, written c.1146:

> The whole of the West and all the barbarian tribes which dwell there had migrated in a body and were marching into Asia through Europe. They were making the journey with all their household, with arms, horses and all the other paraphernalia of war. They were all so zealous and eager that every highroad was full of them. The Frankish soldiers were accompanied by an unarmed host more numerous than the sand or the stars, carrying palms and crosses on their shoulders. Women and children, too, came away from their countries. The sight of them was like many rivers streaming from all sides.

Alexios was so afraid that these Franks might attack the city that he insisted that they must stay in camps outside the city walls. He only allowed leading crusaders to enter, and then only five or six at a time.

Constantinople was home to 500,000 people, making it ten times bigger than the biggest city in western Europe. Bustling markets were filled with food and goods from across the known world and there was a lot of wealth on show. Its churches were marvels of engineering and filled with holy relics as well as magnificent treasures of all sorts. The city's splendour was both impressive and tempting.

The leaders' oaths

Alexios had a particular reason for inviting the leaders into his city. He wanted them to swear an oath of loyalty to him. He was only too aware that his Byzantine rivals might try to use the crusaders to force him off his throne. Besides, he needed to be sure that these Franks would serve him and not their own selfish greed.

There were two parts to the oath that Alexios had devised. The leaders had to promise that they would:

1. become vassals of Alexios, obeying him and doing no harm to his empire – this was similar to the oaths of loyalty that princes were used to making as part of the feudal system
2. return to Alexios any land they might conquer that had previously belonged to his Byzantine Empire.

Persuading the princes to take the oath was not easy. They were among the richest and most powerful men in western Europe. They were not used to answering to anyone! But Alexios was clever. He met with each prince separately when they were without the moral support of the other princes or their armies. He was also lucky: the first group of crusaders to arrive, led by Hugh of Vermandois, was one of the smallest. It was easy to pressurise Hugh into taking the oath. Hugh was the brother of the King of France. Once he had agreed, it was much harder for the others to refuse. One by one, Alexios tried to win them round. The next page shows how four of them responded.

> **Reflect**
>
> What can Anna Komnena's description tell us about:
>
> - the crusaders who reached Constantinople
> - the attitude of the Byzantines to these crusaders?

▲ An eleventh-century Byzantine gold coin showing Emperor Alexios. He wanted these coins to suggest both his wealth and his power

How well did the crusaders deal with the challenges of Asia Minor?

Case study 1: Godfrey of Bouillon

Godfrey of Bouillon was particularly troublesome. He refused several invitations to visit the city and take the oath. He also refused to leave the city and cross the Bosphorus. Frustrated, Alexios made life difficult for Godfrey. He even cut off food supplies for his army. When Godfrey allowed his soldiers to loot neighbouring suburbs and lay siege to one of Alexios's imperial palaces, the emperor's patience snapped. Byzantine troops forcefully subdued Godfrey's crusader army. Realising his army was no match for Alexios's, Godfrey quickly gave in. He took the oath.

Case study 2: Stephen of Blois

Stephen was hosted by Alexios for ten days, during which he was lavished with gifts. He wrote to his wife Adela excitedly:

> The emperor received me worthily and most honourably and lovingly, like a son. He bestowed extensive and very precious gifts on me. In the whole of God's army, there is no duke, no count, or any other important person whom he trusts or favours more than me. In truth, I tell you there is no such man living under heaven today. For he enriches all our princes most generously, consoles the knights with gifts, and restores all the poor with feasts.

Case study 3: Bohemond

Bohemond had spent years fighting the Byzantine Empire in and around southern Italy, so Alexios had to make a particular effort to win him over. He allowed Bohemond to stay in one of the rooms in the palace, where a table was laid out, full of delicacies and food of all kinds. Bohemond suspected a plot to poison him and refused to eat any of the cooked food (although he did give it to his attendants).

Alexios did not give up. He filled a room so full of clothes, gold and silver coins, and gifts that it was almost impossible to get in. When Bohemond saw the room, he was amazed. He was told that everything in it was a present from the emperor. Alexios's generosity paid off: Bohemond took the oath.

Case study 4: Raymond of Toulouse

In the end, only Raymond successfully resisted all Alexios's efforts at persuasion. He agreed to swear to a modified version of the oath where he promised to 'respect' the emperor and his possessions.

Reflect

Why did these crusade leaders each agree to swear an oath to Alexios?

Godfrey of Bouillon rises to his feet after swearing his oath to Alexios, and the gathered crusaders cheer. An oil painting by Alexandre Hesse, 1842

The emperor's assistance

The oath taken by the princes meant that they were committed to serve and obey Alexios. It also meant that the emperor had responsibilities to fulfil for the crusaders. His first move was to give the Franks food and a base across the Bosphorus. This was at Kibotos, where the People's Crusade had been destroyed just eight months earlier. The first crusaders were moved there in February 1097. By May, almost all the crusader groups had reached Constantinople and had moved to Kibotos. The Turks who had crushed the People's Crusade were fighting in another region and left them undisturbed.

Keeping an army of tens of thousands supplied with food was a real challenge. If Alexios failed to provide for them, the crusaders might raid the locality for supplies and make themselves vulnerable. That was what the People's Crusade had done with fatal consequences. Fortunately, Alexios had planned ahead for this official crusade. He had arranged for a huge number of merchants to sell the crusaders wheat, oil, wine and cheese. He had also fixed the prices so that the Franks could not be over-charged by greedy traders.

Advice

Alexios also gave the princes valuable advice. They needed all of his experience and expertise. Much of his advice was about planning for their journey across Asia Minor towards Antioch. Here are some of the main points the emperor made about the daunting land that they must cross:

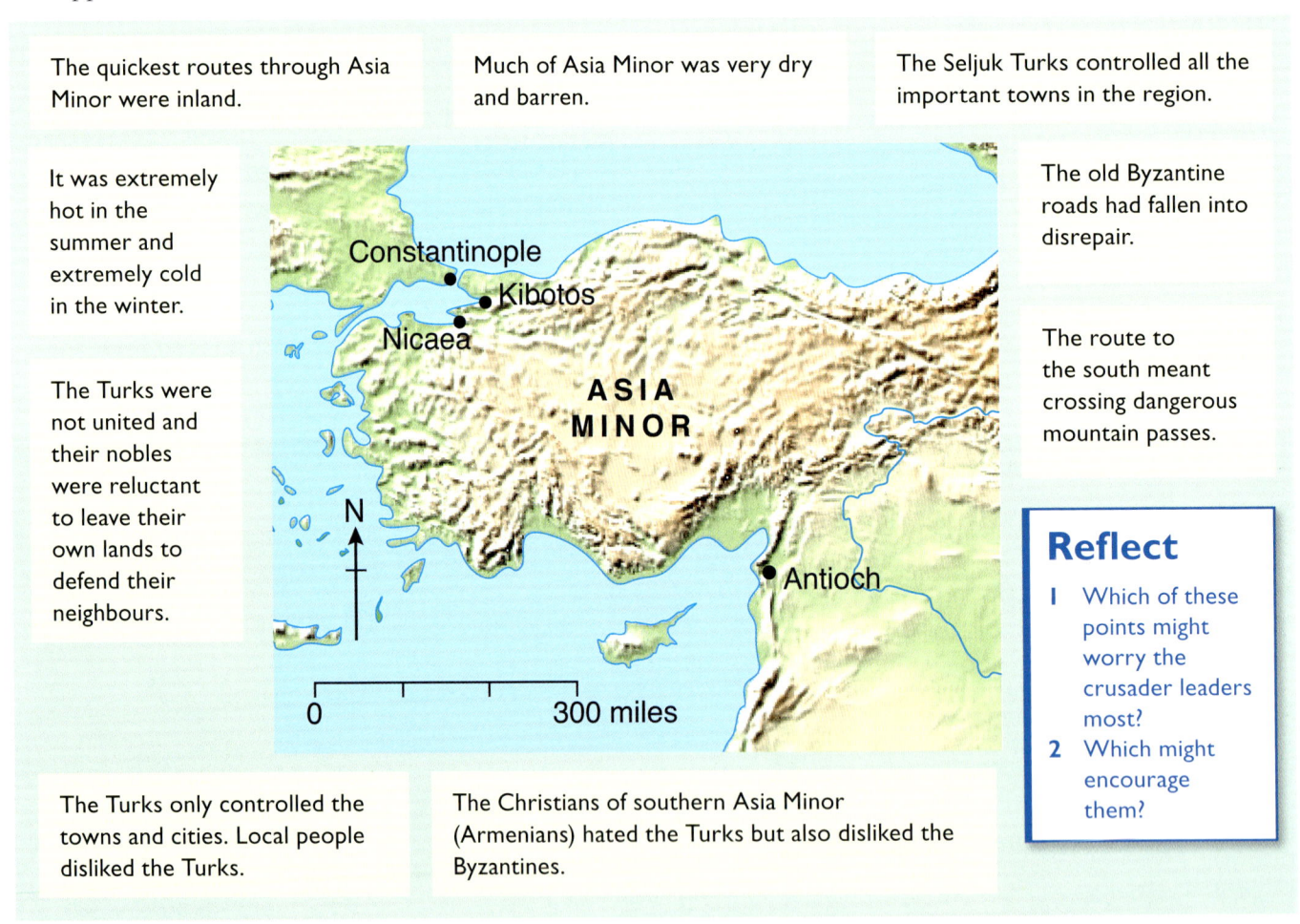

The quickest routes through Asia Minor were inland.

Much of Asia Minor was very dry and barren.

The Seljuk Turks controlled all the important towns in the region.

It was extremely hot in the summer and extremely cold in the winter.

The old Byzantine roads had fallen into disrepair.

The Turks were not united and their nobles were reluctant to leave their own lands to defend their neighbours.

The route to the south meant crossing dangerous mountain passes.

The Turks only controlled the towns and cities. Local people disliked the Turks.

The Christians of southern Asia Minor (Armenians) hated the Turks but also disliked the Byzantines.

Reflect

1. Which of these points might worry the crusader leaders most?
2. Which might encourage them?

Finally, the crusaders gratefully listened to Alexios's valuable advice about how best to fight their Muslim enemy. Most of them had never fought against a Muslim army. According to Anna Komnena in *The Alexiad*, c.1146:

> they were instructed in the methods normally used by the Turks in battle, told how they should draw up a battle line, how to lay ambushes. He advised them not to pursue far when the enemy ran away in flight.

How well did the crusaders deal with the challenges of Asia Minor?

Aims and intentions

The fact that Alexios advised the crusaders in tactics is significant: it shows that he did not intend to travel with them on the crusade. Years later some of the princes claimed that the failure of Alexios to lead them to Jerusalem was a betrayal of his side of the oath. Many crusaders (including the leaders) seem to have expected that Alexios would take over and lead the crusade personally. According to the *Gesta Francorum*, c.1103:

> The emperor for his part swore to come with us, bringing an army and a navy, and faithfully to supply us with provisions both by land and sea, and to take care to restore all those things which we had lost. Moreover he promised that he would not cause or permit anyone to trouble or vex our pilgrims on the way to the Holy Sepulchre.

> **Reflect**
>
> According to the *Gesta Francorum*, what practical help did the crusaders expect Alexios to give them?

It is hard to be sure what Alexios actually promised the crusaders or how he treated them because all the accounts we have were written after the crusade had ended. By this time relations between the western crusaders and the Byzantine Empire had soured badly, with both sides feeling they had been betrayed.

It seems clear, however, that Alexios never had any intention of leading the crusade himself. He was happy to support the crusaders by giving them advice and aid, but only so far as they helped him achieve his own aims of recapturing Byzantine land lost in recent years and in strengthening his control over the empire. For him the crusade was a military campaign driven by his political needs. The Byzantine Church had no doctrine of penance and the idea that the crusade was a religious war with spiritual rewards would have meant little to the emperor. He had no desire to capture Jerusalem. He was also concerned that if he left Constantinople, his rivals there would have an ideal opportunity to seize power.

The differences in understanding and intentions between the emperor and the crusaders caused considerable difficulties in the months that followed.

Motivation

Any early difficulties with Alexios seemed to have been set aside by May 1097. With winter over and with almost all the crusader army in place, the time for action had come. In early May, a large force moved out of Kibotos. This was the moment when Alexios would discover if these crusaders could prove themselves to be a serious army, unlike the rabble that the People's Crusade had been. The emperor promised the crusaders rewards of gold, silver and horses if they could prove their worth as soldiers and recapture from the Turks their first target: the ancient Byzantine city of Nicaea.

> **Record**
>
> Make your first three challenge cards as described on page 45. Your cards should be about these challenges, and how well the crusaders dealt with them:
>
> 1. Avoiding outbreaks of crusader violence and theft at Constantinople
> 2. Establishing a good early relationship with Alexios
> 3. Making the most of Alexios's knowledge and leadership

The siege of Nicaea and the Battle of Dorylaeum

Nicaea was the capital city of the Seljuk Turks. They had controlled it since 1078 and their leader, Sultan Kilij Arslan, was determined to keep it. On the other hand, the city was very important to the crusaders:

1. It was famous to Christians as a place where important early Church councils had been held.
2. It controlled the main routes through Asia Minor. Without it the crusaders had little chance of regaining Asia Minor from the Turks.
3. It was a former Byzantine stronghold and Alexios was determined to recover it.

On 6 May 1097, the crusaders began to gather outside the great walls of the city. It was hard to co-ordinate an army as big as the crusade (between 45,000 and 75,000) and it took nearly six weeks for them to assemble fully. Alexios also sent 2000 Byzantine troops to help with the campaign. Before they were at full strength, the crusaders were vulnerable to attack.

Although the crusade could probably have been destroyed at this point, the Turks did nothing. Having easily defeated the People's Crusade, Kilij Arslan was not afraid of this next wave of crusaders. He had travelled to his eastern lands to sort out a territorial dispute. He left Nicaea defended by just a few thousand Turkish troops. His absence probably saved the crusade from an early disaster.

The defences of Nicaea

Even with relatively few Turks defending the city, the crusaders knew that taking Nicaea would not be easy. Its defences were daunting. The city walls were over ten metres tall with more than a hundred towers arranged at strategic points. There was also a double ditch around the walls. The chronicler Raymond of Aguilers was awestruck by the challenge:

> Nicaea was a city well protected by natural terrain and clever fortifications. Its natural defences consisted of a great lake lapping at its walls and a ditch, brimful of water from nearby streams, blocking the entrance on three sides. Skilful men had enclosed Nicaea with such lofty walls that the city feared neither the attack of enemies not the force of any machine.

On 16 May, Turkish troops sent back to Nicaea by Kilij Arslan poured down from the hills to attack the crusader army. On the same day, the forces of Raymond of Toulouse had reached Nicaea so there were just enough crusaders in place to drive the Turkish troops away.

Reflect

What challenges did the crusaders face in attacking Nicaea?

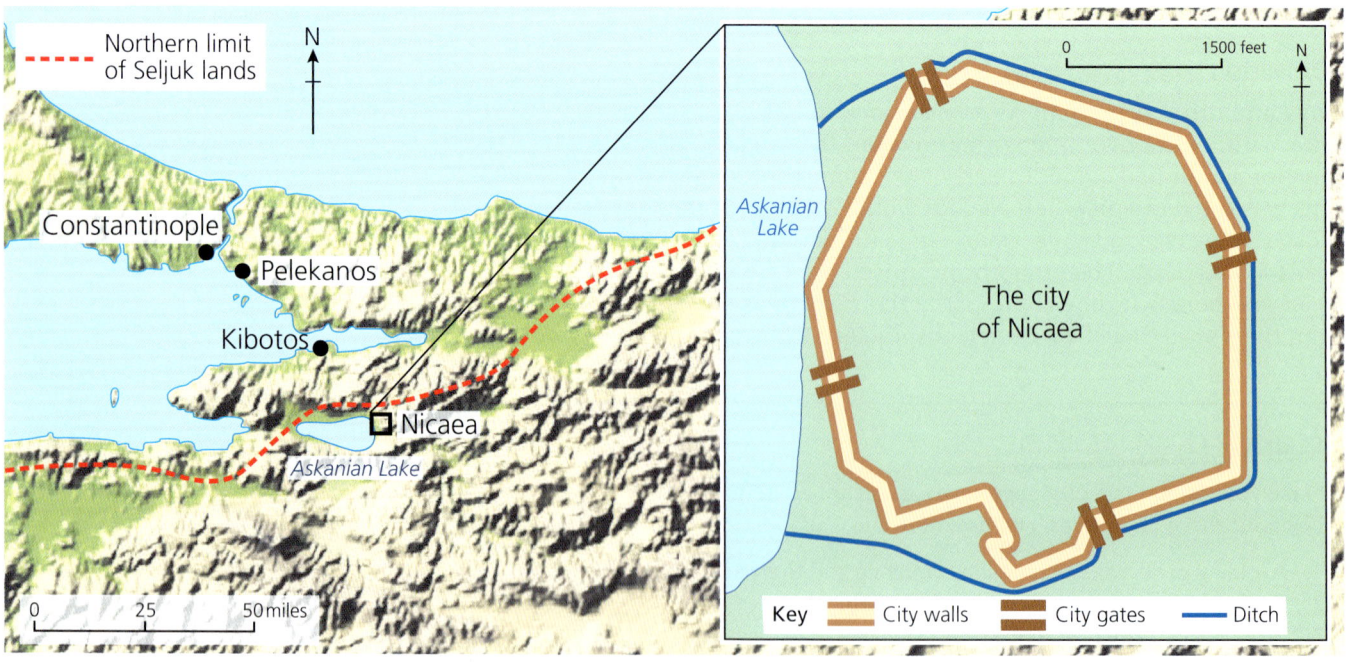

▲ Nicaea and its surroundings, 1097

How well did the crusaders deal with the challenges of Asia Minor?

▼ Remains of the medieval walls and a gateway into Nicaea

The siege begins

Alexios did not travel to Nicaea but he did cross the Bosphorus to Pelekanos from where he could keep in touch with his capital and the campaign. The 2000 Byzantine troops with the Franks were led by Tatikios, one of his best generals. (Some reports say his nose had once been slit in battle so he wore a false one made of solid gold.) Tatikios and the princes formed a leaders' council that worked together to plan the attack on the city.

This council quickly agreed that the crusaders' best weapon, their heavy cavalry, would be of no use against the city's massive walls and defensive ditches. Instead, they decided to rely on a siege. This involved:

- a blockade – the city was surrounded on its landward side, cutting off roads and supply routes
- an assault – the crusaders attacked the city's huge walls, hoping to breach them or scale them.

At first the crusaders attacked the walls from simple ladders and launched rocks from catapults. The Turks used ballistae (similar to huge crossbows) to hurl stones at the enemy while their archers cut down crusaders as they approached the walls. Those who did reach the walls faced a barrage of rocks and burning pitch and oil, hurled from above by the defenders.

The crusaders tried psychological warfare too: they fired into the city the severed heads of Turkish soldiers killed on 16 May. The Turks retaliated by lowering giant iron hooks to haul up the bodies of dead crusaders from the foot of the walls, leaving them hanging out to rot.

▲ The siege of Nicaea from a thirteenth-century manuscript

▲ Godfrey of Bouillon leads a crusader attack on the walls of Nicaea. From a fourteenth-century French manuscript

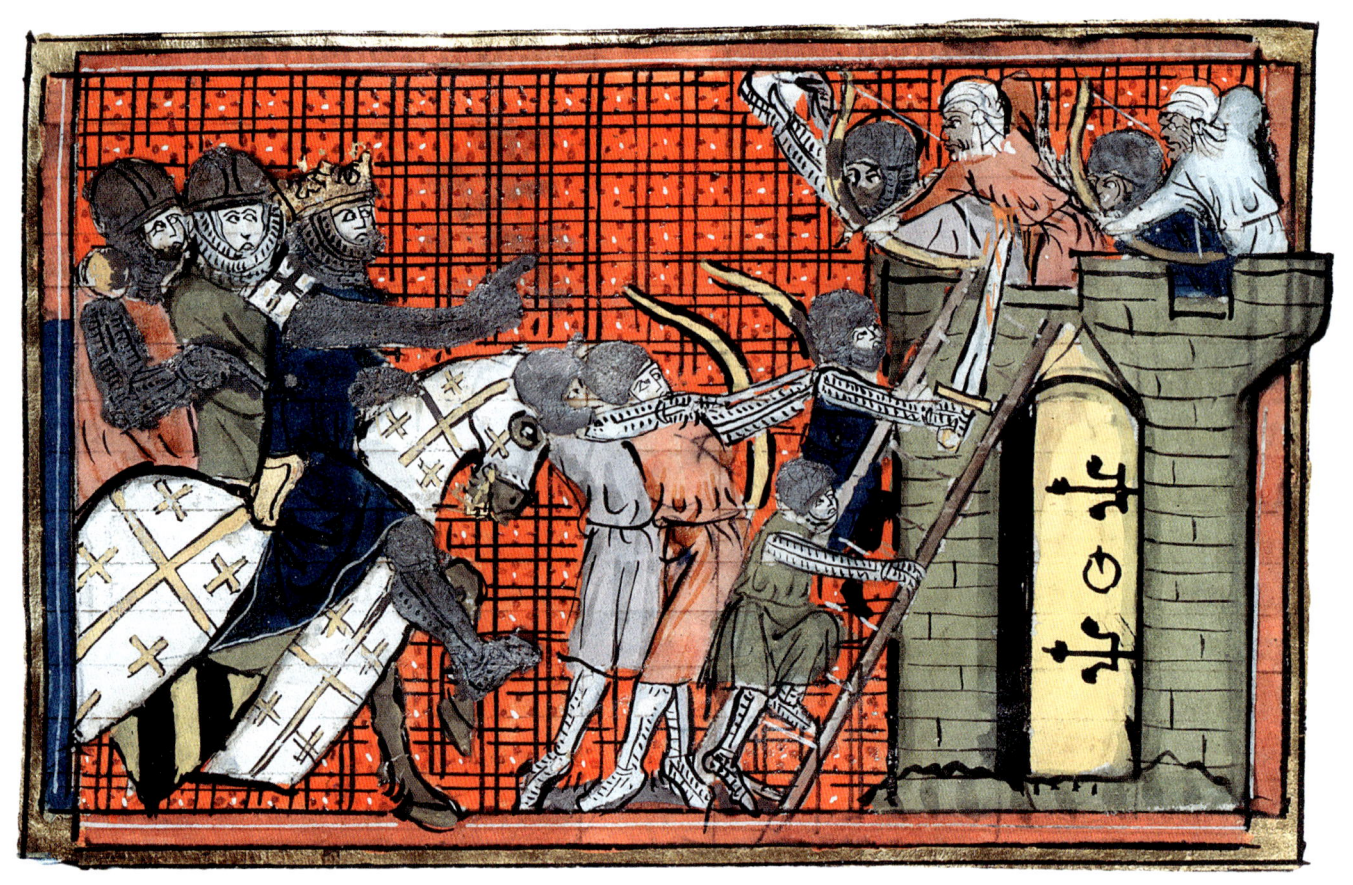

Siege engines

The siege exposed the crusaders to the risk of starvation as the countryside could not support an army the size of the crusade for long. They worked hard to improve their weaponry. The author of the *Gesta Francorum* recorded that:

> On the day of the Lord's Ascension [c.20 May, 1097] we began to attack the city on all sides and to construct machines made of wood and wooden towers with which we might be able to destroy towers on the city walls. We attacked so bravely and fiercely that we even undermined its wall.

Some of Raymond of Toulouse's troops used timber from forests near Nicaea to build a testudo (tortoise). This strong, slope-roofed mobile screen allowed a team of sappers to undermine a tower on the southern wall. On 1 June a small section of the wall collapsed. But the Turks worked frantically through the night and, to the crusaders' dismay, by the next morning the wall had been rebuilt.

One group of knights built a rugged shelter made of massive oak beams, under which crusaders could advance in safety to try to bore a hole in the walls. Unfortunately, on its first use it collapsed, crushing twenty crusaders to death. Building really effective siege equipment was highly skilled work and it seems that the crusaders at Nicaea lacked either the time, talent or both to make effective siege engines.

In his 1997 book, *Latin Siege Warfare in the Twelfth Century*, historian Randall Rogers argues that:

> Although the Gesta Francorum mentions wooden towers and other wooden devices, the short period of construction involved and the description of the attack make it very doubtful that wall-dominating siege towers were employed. Rather, armoured shelters and roofs and probably artillery were employed in this assault. This does not remove the possibility that the construction of siege towers was undertaken but not completed by the time of the city's surrender.

Reflect

Look again at the *Gesta Francorum* source and the interpretations given in the picture above and by Randall Rogers. How useful are these for a historian studying the siege of Nicaea?

As the weeks went by, it became obvious that the city could not be taken through a long siege. The city's walls were just too big and the Turks could easily bring supplies into Nicaea across the Askanian Lake. The council of leaders met on 10 June to discuss the situation. They came up with a daring new plan.

How well did the crusaders deal with the challenges of Asia Minor?

The city falls

The city's weakest defences faced the Askanian Lake. An attack by ship might be able to breach the walls. As there was no river big enough to carry the crusaders' ships to the lake, the ships would have to be carried overland, a distance of 20 miles.

The princes wrote to Alexios with their new plan. He agreed to help them and the crusaders set about building special oxen-drawn carts to transport the ships which finally arrived at the shores of the Askanian Lake on 17 June.

At dawn the next day, the attack began. Trumpeters and drummers created a terrifying racket. While the crusaders attacked the city's walls, Byzantine forces attacked from the lake, with hundreds of banners and standards crammed onto the ships to make it appear that there were far more attackers than there actually were. Seeing what they took for a huge force approaching across the lake, the Turks surrendered. But not to the Franks.

The previous day Alexios had secretly sent an envoy into the city to negotiate its surrender. He offered the Turks protection and gifts of money. Faced with a huge crusader army camp outside their walls and fearing Frankish brutality, the Turks agreed to Alexios's terms. Alexios was afraid that the crusaders would never accept this surrender so he staged the attack from the Askanian Lake knowing that the Turks would allow his men to enter the city. As the crusaders kept up their land attack, to their surprise they saw Alexios's standard already fluttering on top of the city's walls.

▶ A Byzantine naval battle, from an eleventh-century manuscript

A triumph?

The victory at Nicaea seemed to be a remarkable success for the crusaders. In only six weeks they had worked with the Byzantines to capture a city believed to be unbreakable. Unfortunately, the close co-operation did not last.

Despite their success, there were ominous signs for the crusade. After going behind the crusaders' backs to negotiate a secret deal with the Turks, Alexios gave his soldiers orders to shut its gates once they had taken control. The Byzantines kept the Franks outside.

Unsurprisingly, many crusaders were angry that they had been denied the final victory and the plunder that came with it. Alexios moved quickly to calm them, making generous gifts of gold and silver to the princes and leading knights, as well as copper coins to the foot soldiers. His authority and his wealth kept order.

The reaction of the Muslim world

The Muslim world was deeply shocked by the fall of Nicaea. If the crusaders could capture such a mighty fortress in just six weeks, then who knew what else they were capable of? A Muslim in Damascus fretted:

> There began to arrive a succession of reports that the armies of the Franks had appeared from the direction of the sea of Constantinople with forces not to be reckoned for multitude … as reports grew and spread from mouth to mouth far and wide, the people grew anxious and disturbed in mind.

Record

Make your next three challenge cards as described on page 45. Your cards should be about these challenges:

1. Surviving in the camp at Kibotos where the People's Crusade had been wiped out
2. Capturing the city of Nicaea
3. Strengthening the leadership of the crusade

The Battle of Dorylaeum

After taking Nicaea, the crusaders rested for a week then prepared to continue their journey. The plan was that the Franks, supported by the local knowledge of Tatikios and a small force of Byzantine troops, would cross Asia Minor, heading south-eastwards (see map on page 45). Alexios would follow to hold whatever towns the crusaders won and to restore Byzantine control of his lost lands, just as he had wished. There were, however, two unavoidable problems:

1. It would be hard to supply the crusader force of about 70,000 people as it was on the move.
2. Alexios would no longer be with them to give his authority and leadership.

These two problems dogged the crusade over the next few weeks.

The decision to divide

Everyone knew that it would be very difficult to supply such an enormous crusade. The local markets in Asia Minor could not possibly provide food for so many people on the move. This meant that the crusaders would have to rely on foraging across the local countryside. Even that would barely feed everyone. Because of this, the crusade's council of leaders made a risky decision. They split the crusade into two groups. They would follow much the same route but could move more easily in two groups and could forage slightly different areas. They agreed to stay in close contact by messenger.

The two crusader forces left Nicaea on 29 June 1097. They were heading for an abandoned military camp several days' march away at Dorylaeum. The first group was led by Bohemond, Tatikios, Robert of Normandy and Stephen of Blois. They were joined by Robert of Flanders, whose crusaders had arrived at Nicaea in early June. They travelled about two miles ahead of the second group, led by Godfrey of Bouillon, Raymond of Toulouse and Hugh of Vermandois.

The Turks attack

Although Kilij Arslan had been forced to abandon Nicaea he had not given up. After gathering his forces, he tracked the crusaders as they crossed his lands.

On 30 June, Bohemond noticed some Turks in the surrounding hills and sent word to the second group of crusaders as his own force made camp in a valley some miles north of Dorylaeum. But early on 1 July, it was still a shock to hear the terrifying war cry of the Turks, cutting through the dawn air. To their horror, the leading group of crusaders realised they had been surrounded by 10,000 Turkish horsemen. As they drew ever closer, these Turks rained a cloud of arrows on the terrified Franks.

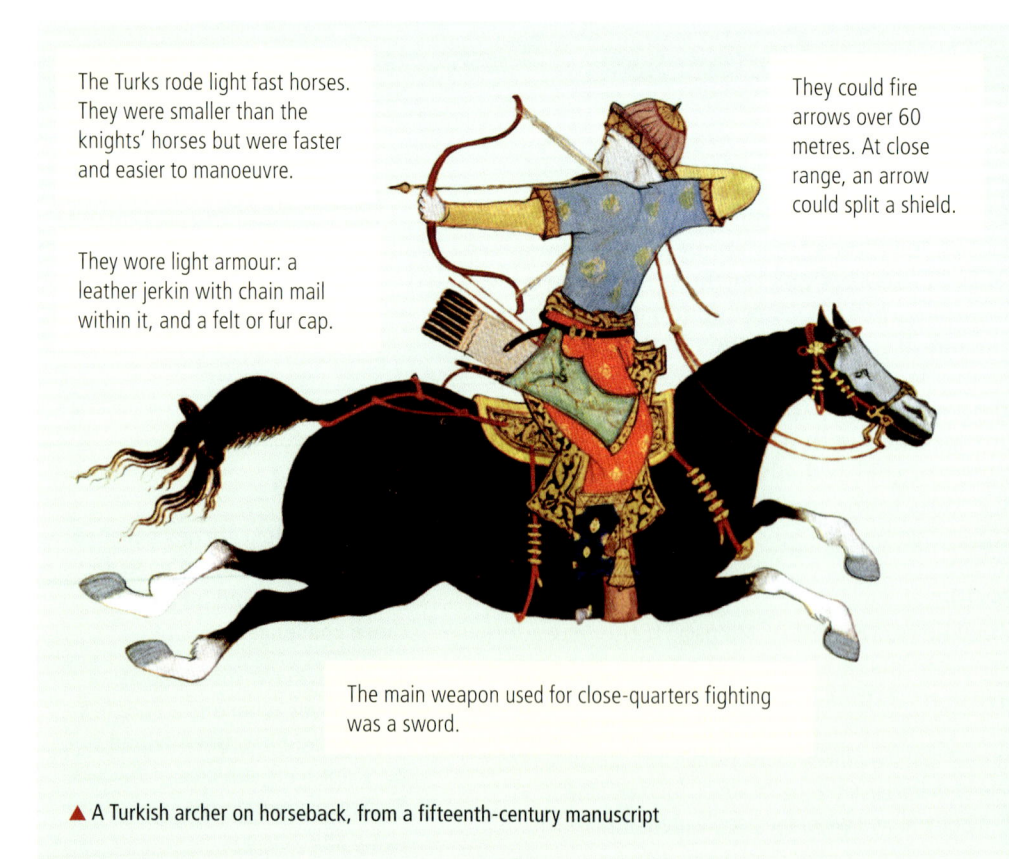

The Turks rode light fast horses. They were smaller than the knights' horses but were faster and easier to manoeuvre.

They wore light armour: a leather jerkin with chain mail within it, and a felt or fur cap.

They could fire arrows over 60 metres. At close range, an arrow could split a shield.

The main weapon used for close-quarters fighting was a sword.

▲ A Turkish archer on horseback, from a fifteenth-century manuscript

Turkish warfare

Turks preferred fighting at speed on open ground. They loved to ambush their enemy, surround them and fire a cloud of arrows into their ranks to demoralise them and break their formation. As their enemy panicked, the Turks would then charge in to fight at close quarters. If necessary, they would use the tactic of a feigned retreat: pretending to withdraw in order to lure some of the enemy away from their formation before turning and attacking them.

> **Reflect**
>
> How were Turkish cavalry different from the knights of western Europe?

How well did the crusaders deal with the challenges of Asia Minor?

Terror

The chronicler Fulcher of Chartres found himself trapped in the middle of the camp with other non-combatants. Years later he recalled:

> The Turks were howling like wolves and furiously shooting a cloud of arrows. We were stunned by this. Since we faced death and since many of us were wounded we soon took to flight. This is not remarkable because to all of us such warfare was unknown … We were all indeed huddled together like sheep in a fold, trembling and frightened, surrounded on all sides by enemies so that we could not turn in any direction. It was clear to us that this had happened because of our sins. A great clamour rose, not only from our men and our women and children but also from the pagans rushing upon us. By now we had no hope of surviving.

Survival

Sure enough, many crusaders did die, mainly among stragglers who were cut off from the main camp group. But after about six hours of bloody battle, the crusade survived. They won an unlikely victory that ended any further attacks from Kilij Arslan. The crusaders themselves were convinced they had been saved by God. Historians today prefer to give reasons such as these:

- Bohemond acted wisely. He had made camp by a marsh that gave some protection against the Turkish horsemen. He quickly moved non-combatants and equipment into the centre and formed a tight defensive formation around it.
- Bohemond and Robert of Normandy led 700 knights out to confront the enemy.
- The knights were forced back to the camp and began to panic until they were rallied by Robert of Normandy and Bohemond. The call went out: 'Stand fast together, trusting in Christ and in the victory of the Holy Cross. Today, please God, you will all gain much booty.'
- Kilij Arslan had counted on the crusaders panicking. Instead the Turks found themselves drawn into close-quarters combat, where they could not take advantage of their speed and archery skills.
- At one point in the battle, the Turks broke into the camp but the foot soldiers fought doggedly and the camp was never over-run.
- After five hours, reinforcements from the second group arrived at midday. With no time to draw up in formation they rode straight into battle.
- Faced with the full crusader army, the Turks began to retreat. Their camp was ransacked, and running battles continued as the crusaders chased the retreating Turks.

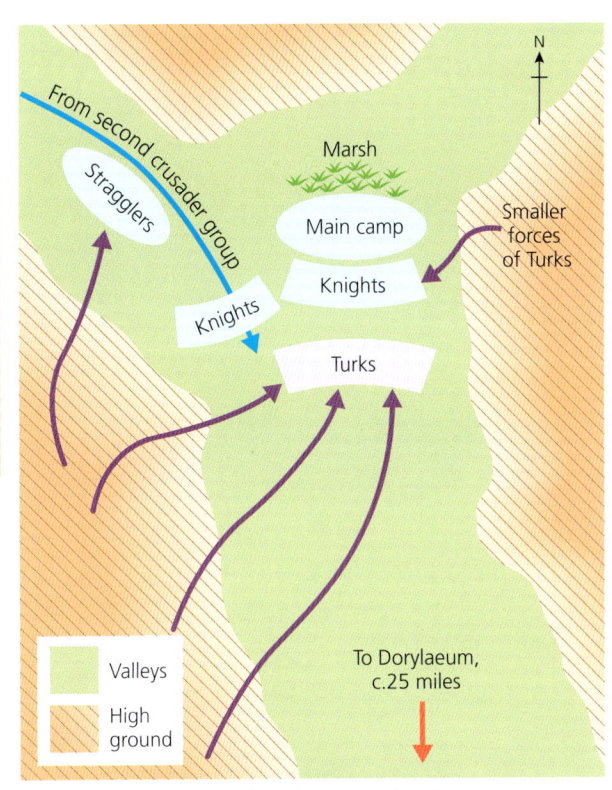

▲ Positions at the Battle of Dorylaeum, 1 July 1097

Reflect

Look at the reasons given for the crusaders' survival (left). Which are to do with:

- strong leadership
- tactics
- crusader motivation and determination
- Turkish mistakes?

Record

Make your next two challenge cards as described on page 45. Your cards should be about these challenges and how well the crusaders dealt with them:

1. Coping with moving and feeding such an enormous group of crusaders
2. Fighting the Turks in open battle near Dorylaeum

The journey across Asia Minor

The Battle of Dorylaeum was a costly victory for the crusaders. Historians estimate that 3000 Turks and 4000 Christians were killed. The crusaders took three days to bury their dead and rest before they continued their journey across Asia Minor. This time they travelled as a single group.

▲ The dry plateau of central Anatolia with mountains nearby

Over the Anatolian plateau

This stage of the journey took the crusaders deep into Turkish territory, moving them ever further from the relative safety of the Byzantine Empire and secure supply lines. To avoid certain Turkish strongholds, the crusaders followed a route across the Anatolian plateau. This was a high, harsh landscape at the heart of Asia Minor. In the scorching summer heat, it was almost completely dry. It was impossible to supply the entire army by foraging in such a barren land. To make matters worse, as he had retreated Kilij Arslan had devastated the countryside, destroying what little food and water supplies there were.

Just four days after leaving Dorylaeum, crusaders and their animals were dying of thirst. The *Gesta Francorum* describes the horrific conditions the crusaders endured:

> We barely emerged or escaped alive, for we suffered greatly from hunger and thirst, and found nothing to eat except prickly plants which we gathered and rubbed between our hands. On such food we survived wretchedly enough, but we lost most of our horses, so that many of our knights had to go on as foot soldiers, and for lack of horses we had to use oxen as mounts and our great need compelled us to use goats, sheep and dogs as beasts of burden.

Remarkably, the chronicler, Fulcher of Chartres, who was with the crusade at this time, reported that morale was still high after the victory at Dorylaeum. It is certainly true that the crusaders made rapid progress through Anatolia:

- **Early August 1097:** The crusaders reached the fertile region of Pisidia. They were able to rest and recover their strength. Some nobles even went hunting and Godrey of Bouillon was mauled by a bear but survived.
- **Mid-August 1097:** The crusaders reached the oasis of Iconium. The Turkish garrison there had fled. Raymond of Toulouse, who had fallen seriously ill, quickly recovered once at the oasis.
- **Late August 1097:** The crusade reached Heraclea where a Turkish garrison resisted briefly before retreating. A comet appeared in the sky and the crusaders took this as a sign of God's favour.

Reflect

What might have made the crusaders so sure that God was favouring them by August 1097?

How well did the crusaders deal with the challenges of Asia Minor?

The two routes to Antioch

In mid-September, the crusaders left Heraclea. Their next target was the great city of Antioch in northern Syria.

Before they had travelled far, the leaders decided that they should once again split into two separate groups: a small group led by Baldwin of Boulogne, the younger brother of Godfrey of Bouillon, headed south into the region of Cilicia; the main crusade took a longer route, capturing towns near Caesarea.

The Cilician expedition

Baldwin led a force of some 500 troops and was soon followed by Bohemond's nephew Tancred, accompanied by 200 men. Tancred left without consulting the crusade's leadership. Together, they were taking the shortest and fastest way to Antioch, but this led them through the narrow mountain pass known as the Cilician Gate (see map). Such narrow routes were easy to defend and the Turks might easily have been able to attack and destroy this relatively small group of knights as they made their way through the pass.

In fact, the crusaders made their way through the pass in safety and pressed on towards Tarsus, the most important town in the region. At first sight everything that followed seems to show some very positive outcomes but, in reality, there were also some very disturbing developments.

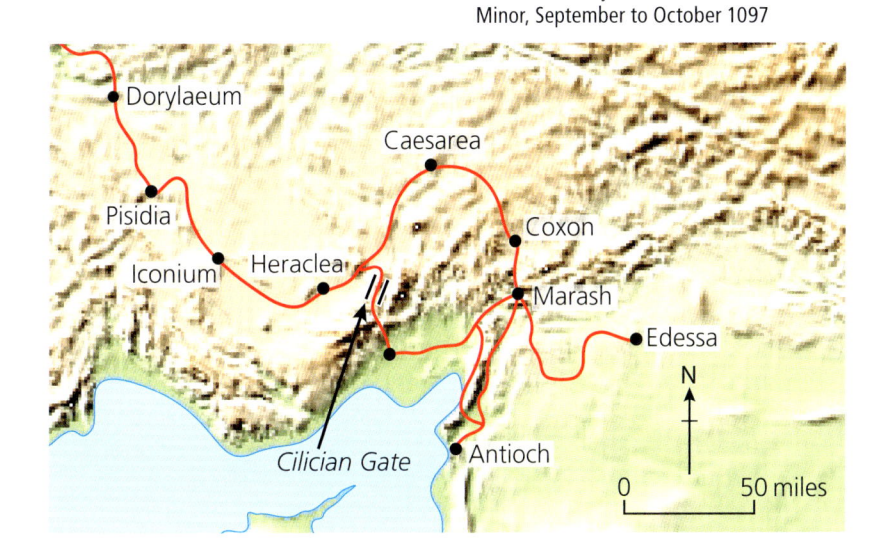

▼ Routes taken by the crusaders across Asia Minor, September to October 1097

Positive outcomes

- By the end of September, all of Cilicia was regained from the Turks. Its people were Christians (of the type known as Armenians) and so they were grateful to the western crusaders for ending Muslim rule and were ready to help them in the coming months.
- By taking Tarsus and other important towns and ports in Cilicia, the crusaders had opened good foraging land and sea routes that helped to supply their needs.
- Alexios was grateful that a wealthy and important part of the Byzantine Empire had been regained from the Turks.

Disturbing developments

- Tancred's unauthorised decision to break away from the main crusade to track Baldwin's force into Cilicia may have been due to personal rivalry and jealousy: whoever took Cilicia would gain favour with Alexios and might even win the lordship of the area.
- Baldwin was the brother of Godfrey of Bouillon and some historians believe that Godfrey's rival Bohemond sent his nephew Tancred to make sure that their family won a share of any rewards for taking Cilicia. Personal jealousies could be made worse by family rivalries.
- During the campaign in Cilicia, Tancred felt humiliated and infuriated by Baldwin. At one point, two groups of their knights drew each other's blood and several were killed. The unity of the crusade was showing serious signs of disintegration.

> **Reflect**
>
> Would you describe the Cilician expedition as a success?

The route of the main crusade

While Tancred and Baldwin headed into Cilicia, the rest of the crusade took the longer route northwards through the region of Cappadocia before turning south-east again. Although this was not the most direct route to Antioch, there was a good reason for going the long way round. The crusaders hoped to win over the local Armenian population. Not only would they gain allies, they could cut off their target, the city of Antioch, from outside aid. The crusaders' route is shown on the map on page 57.

The crusaders found the first part of their journey easy enough. They were welcomed by the local Armenian population, who hoped that the crusaders would free them from the Turks. Sure enough, the Franks regained the important towns of Caesarea and Coxon. The Turkish garrisons increasingly offered little resistance, sometimes fleeing before the crusaders' approach. At one Armenian town, the people appointed one of the Frankish knights as its new governor.

In this first part of their journey, the crusaders made quick progress and found plentiful supplies in the rich towns along their way. It was when they left the safety of the plain and the rich towns behind them that their real troubles began. The autumn rains had arrived, washing away what little remained of the already narrow and dangerous path over the Anti-Taurus mountain range. No one dared risk riding their horses on the slippery paths which fell away into steep ravines. They watched in horror as their pack animals, roped together, stumbled and slipped in the mud, dragging other animals over the precipice with them. The writer of the *Gesta Francorum* (c.1103) records how the crusaders were in despair:

> We began to cross a damnable mountain, which was so high and steep that none of our men dared to overtake another on the mountain path. Horses fell over the precipice, and one beast of burden dragged another down. As for the knights, they stood about in a great state of gloom, wringing their hands because they were so frightened and miserable, not knowing what to do with themselves and their armour, and offering to sell their shields, valuable breastplates and helmets for threepence or fivepence or any price they could get. Those who could not find a buyer threw their arms away and went on.

Finally, in mid-October 1097, the crusade arrived at Marash. The crusaders were welcomed by the Armenians and rested a few days.

▼ A high pass in the Anti-Taurus mountains, just above the town of Marash. When the many thousands of cold and hungry crusaders struggled over this pass, the bare slopes turned to mud

How well did the crusaders deal with the challenges of Asia Minor?

Baldwin and Edessa

In mid-October, the main crusade set off once again for Antioch. Tancred and his force joined them having taken a southern route out of Cilicia. Baldwin, on the other hand, had marched his force east and arrived at Marash while the main crusade was still resting there. Unlike Tancred, he was no longer heading for Antioch. He had plans of his own. Accompanied by at least 80 knights, he headed east towards the Armenian principality of Edessa. It seems that Thoros, the ruler of Edessa, had heard of Baldwin's successes in Cilicia and had invited him to fight the Turks in his area.

As Baldwin approached Edessa, Armenian populations rose up against the local Turkish garrisons. The Turkish troops either fled or were massacred. By the winter of 1097, Baldwin had captured lands up to the River Euphrates. Once it became clear he was in no rush to move on to Edessa, Thoros made a new offer: he promised to adopt Baldwin as his son and heir and share power with him. This was enough to persuade Baldwin to continue his journey to Edessa, and he arrived in February 1098. He was greeted with great joy by Thoros and the Armenians. In an elaborate adoption ceremony, both men were stripped to the waist before a shirt was placed over both their heads and they rubbed their chests against each other. At the end of the ceremony Baldwin had officially become the son of Thoros.

Thoros was unpopular among his people and before long a group of conspirators tried to capture him. He was caught and ripped to pieces by an enraged crowd. The next day, Baldwin, who had ignored pleas for help from his 'father', was made the new Count of Edessa.

Some historians say that Baldwin was breaking the oath he made to Alexios by taking land that he had promised to return to the emperor. Others say that he took Edessa with Alexios's approval. Either way, Baldwin had:

- diverted from the main crusade without the agreement of its leaders
- deprived the main force of at least 80 knights
- brought shame on the crusade among Christians who deplored his failure to help Thoros.

He had, however, won a personal prize as the ruler of the first Frankish state in the east.

Reflect

Do you think Baldwin's actions at Edessa can be called a success for the crusade?

◀ The people of Edessa pay homage to their new king, Baldwin I. From a thirteenth-century manuscript

Record

Make your final three challenge cards as described on page 45. Your cards should be about these challenges:

1. Crossing Anatolia
2. Capturing Cilicia
3. Getting the full force of crusaders out of Asia Minor and ready to press south

Review

1. Look back at all your challenge cards. Make any additions and amendments that you think may be needed now that you know more of what happened later in the crusaders' journey across Asia Minor.
2. Arrange the cards on a surface so that any that have common themes are close together.
3. Arrange the cards with challenges that were successfully dealt with at the top and challenges that the crusaders failed to deal with at the bottom.
4. Overall, how well do you think the crusaders dealt with the challenges of Asia Minor?

CLOSER LOOK 3

The art of siege warfare

It may sound simple to lay siege to a town or city. Surely all it involves is sealing off any entrances, standing guard to stop food reaching the inhabitants, and waiting until hunger makes them surrender? But that sort of blockade may take months and has its own dangers as the crusaders found out. In reality, sieges were very complex and might involve all sorts of strategies, depending on the exact circumstances.

Historian Jim Bradbury has suggested a list of what he called 'the six Ss' to describe how a siege might be made to work. These are:

1. **Subverting** the defenders. This might involve persuading the ruler of the city to hand over his town and maybe change sides, or possibly bribing someone else on the inside to open a gate or allow attackers to get inside.
2. **Scaring** the defenders. They might be intimidated by the actual (or pretend) size of the attacking army, or psychological warfare might be used such as launching severed heads over the walls. It might also rely on building up a reputation for brutal slaughter of inhabitants in cities that refused to surrender.
3. **Storming** the gates and walls. This might cost many lives. The attackers needed large numbers of soldiers who were prepared to scale the walls on ladders or smash the gates with battering rams. These might be iron-tipped tree trunks, swinging below a strong timber shelter on wheels. This would be rolled up to the gates. Another siege machine that protected the attackers was the siege tower, a tall structure often on wheels. It was covered in animal hides that were fairly light but stopped enemy arrows. After levelling the ground, the tower could be wheeled up to the walls. Soldiers would climb up inside of the tower, drop a drawbridge onto the walls and fight their way across.
4. **Sapping** (or mining) below the defensive walls of the castle or town. This is also called 'undermining'. The sappers or miners would either approach the walls by making a long-distance tunnel or by sheltering below a sturdy timber-framed mobile cover. Either way, they hoped to be protected from the missiles, hot oil or fire that would certainly be rained down on them from the defenders. As they dug below the foundations of the wall, they would prop up their tunnel with strong, wooden props. When all was ready, they would start a fire in the hole, often ensuring that it burned at a great heat by adding a dead pig to the bonfire. The flames would consume the props and the wall would fall.

▼ A siege shown in a fourteenth-century manuscript. The men on the right might be discussing their siege strategy!

▼ A siege shown in a twentieth-century children's magazine called *Look and Learn*

The art of siege warfare

5. **'Shelling'** the walls and the buildings inside the town. This could be done with a variety of siege engines. Some were really powerful and could hurl enormous rocks with a fair degree of accuracy. Others were lighter but could still sling large stones and other missiles at or over the walls. The forces involved meant that these machines or 'engines' needed to be built by experienced and skilled engineers, working with timber, iron and rope.
6. **Starvation**. This needed patience and the confidence that the attacking force would be able to keep itself fed and watered as it surrounded the town. It was really hard to seal off all entrances to large towns or cities so the defenders could often get supplies despite being besieged. The other problem was that attackers might themselves come under attack from a relief force arriving to help those in the city. Trapped between the walls of the town and the army arriving behind them, they could be wiped out in a very short time.

Siege warfare can be very dramatic, which is maybe why artists down the ages have loved to illustrate it with their own interpretations. These pages show examples in images from the fourteenth, nineteenth and twentieth centuries.

Reflect

1. Which of the six siege strategies listed here can you see in the images on these pages?
2. How many of these siege strategies did the crusaders use at Nicaea and Antioch?

▶ A siege shown in a nineteenth-century engraving by Gustav Doré

4 'The greatest test'
Why did it take the crusaders so long to capture the city of Antioch?

▲ The ancient city of Antioch with steep mountains in the background. An engraving made in 1860

After weeks of marching across the treacherous Anti-Taurus mountains, on 20 October 1097, the crusaders finally reached the ancient Syrian city of Antioch. This engraving was made over 700 years after the First Crusade, but it gives a strong sense of the city and its surroundings.

Antioch had once been the third largest city in the Roman Empire. Its location made it an important trading station between east and west. Lying at the edge of a fertile plain with access to coastal ports, the city grew rich and was a vibrant cultural and economic centre. Over the centuries it became home to people of different religious faiths.

Antioch's success lay partly in its secure geographical position. The River Orontes provided a barrier to any invaders approaching either from the coast or through the mountain passes to the north and east. Most people lived on the level ground near the river but, high above them, there was a fortified citadel and a natural water supply. Enormous thick walls surrounded the whole complex.

The Byzantine Empire had lost this city to the Turks in 1084. The crusaders had come to take it back. They had taken Nicaea in under six weeks. Surely it would not take long to capture Antioch?

Reflect

In the engraving find:

1. the ruins of Antioch's old walls stretching high up the mountains and behind the city
2. the River Orontes flowing in front of the city and then behind a slope in the foreground.

Why did it take the crusaders so long to capture the city of Antioch?

Why bother with Antioch?

The crusaders could have by-passed Antioch and continued to march southwards to Jerusalem. It is not obvious why they would choose to spend time and energy attacking a city that was so well-protected by natural geographical features and strong man-made defences.

It is true that Antioch was an important trading and cultural centre, but there were other equally important Syrian cities that the crusaders did not attack such as Aleppo and Damascus. Why then, did they bother with Antioch?

Historians have given several main reasons for the crusaders' attack on Antioch:

1. Antioch's real significance for the crusaders lay not in its economic or political position, but in its role in the history of Christianity. The first churches in Antioch were established by St Peter within a few years of Christ's death.
2. Antioch lay on a direct Christian pilgrimage route to Jerusalem. If the crusaders were going to reclaim Jerusalem for Christendom, and ensure a safe passage for Christians travelling through Syria in the future, they would have to wrestle Antioch back from the Turks.
3. Antioch was one of the most important prizes desired by Emperor Alexios. It had been lost from his empire very recently and he wanted it back. The crusade leaders had taken an oath to serve him.

If they had known how hard it would be to take the city, the crusaders might have passed it by! When they left Nicaea in June, Stephen of Blois had written to his wife telling her that the crusaders hoped to be in Jerusalem within five weeks unless Antioch proved to be a stumbling block. Since then, it had taken the crusaders twelve weeks simply to reach Antioch. They were to spend a further year and a half securing the city. In that time they would survive a desperate siege, fight a massive pitched battle against a much stronger force and become embroiled in rivalries which almost tore the crusade apart. These difficulties were so severe compared with anything that the crusaders experienced before or later, that historian Jonathan Phillips has called the capture of Antioch their 'greatest test'.

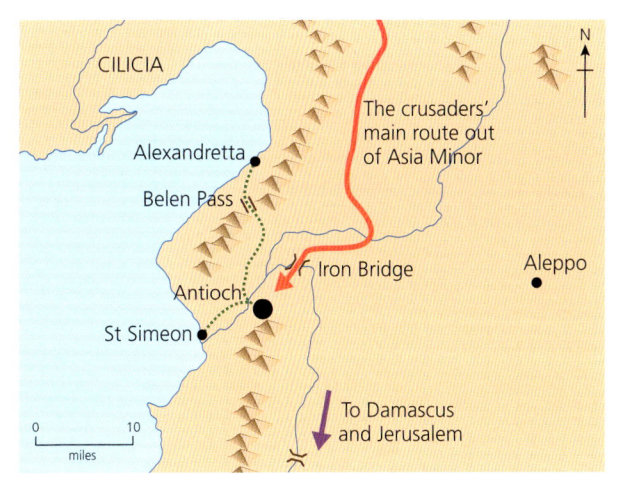

▲ Antioch and its position in northern Syria

Reflect
Which of these three reasons do you think would have mattered most to the crusader leaders?

The Enquiry

The story of how the crusaders eventually managed to capture and control Antioch is full of twists and turns. You will learn what happened in these three stages:

1. **The siege of Antioch** – how the crusaders tried to blockade the city.
2. **The capture of the city** – how the crusaders eventually entered the city.
3. **The defeat of Kerbogha** – how the crusaders defeated the Turkish army that trapped them in the city.

This time your enquiry question actually involves two challenges in one. You need to understand:

a) why the city could not be taken quickly, and
b) why, despite those difficulties, it was eventually taken by the crusaders.

To organise your ideas and evidence, create an explanation timeline based on the one shown here.

Reasons for delay	Date and event	Reasons for survival and success

Record

Start making the first section of your explanation timeline (see page 63). At the top of this section use the heading **'The siege of Antioch, November to December 1097'**.

The siege of Antioch

To reach the city walls of Antioch, the crusaders first had to fight their way over the 'Iron Bridge' about twelve miles north-east of the city. The bridge had enormous iron-clad gates and controlled a vital crossing over the River Orontes (see map on page 63 and on this page).

As the huge crusader force appeared, Antioch's inhabitants took refuge inside the city's strong walls. The Franks settled into the positions shown on the map below. The princes quickly decided that a full-scale assault was completely impractical and that they must mount a siege. But even this would not be easy, as the plan below shows.

The overall length of the walls (three miles in total) meant that it was virtually impossible for any invading army to completely encircle the city.

The Turks had constant supplies of water from springs and streams.

The crusaders could not shut off the 'Iron Gate' in the city walls as it was inaccessible in the mountains. The Turks could always smuggle in supplies of food and could send and receive messages. The city was never fully cut off.

The imposing city walls, up to twenty metres high and two metres thick in places, made it virtually impossible to get inside the city.

The Turks could rain arrows and other missiles down on any attackers who even approached the walls.

There were six main gates within the city walls. All were heavily guarded by Turkish soldiers.

The Bridge Gate controlled the only way over the River Orontes and the only road out to the nearest port at St Simeon. It was so close to the city walls that the Turks could do terrible harm to any crusaders who approached this vital crossing.

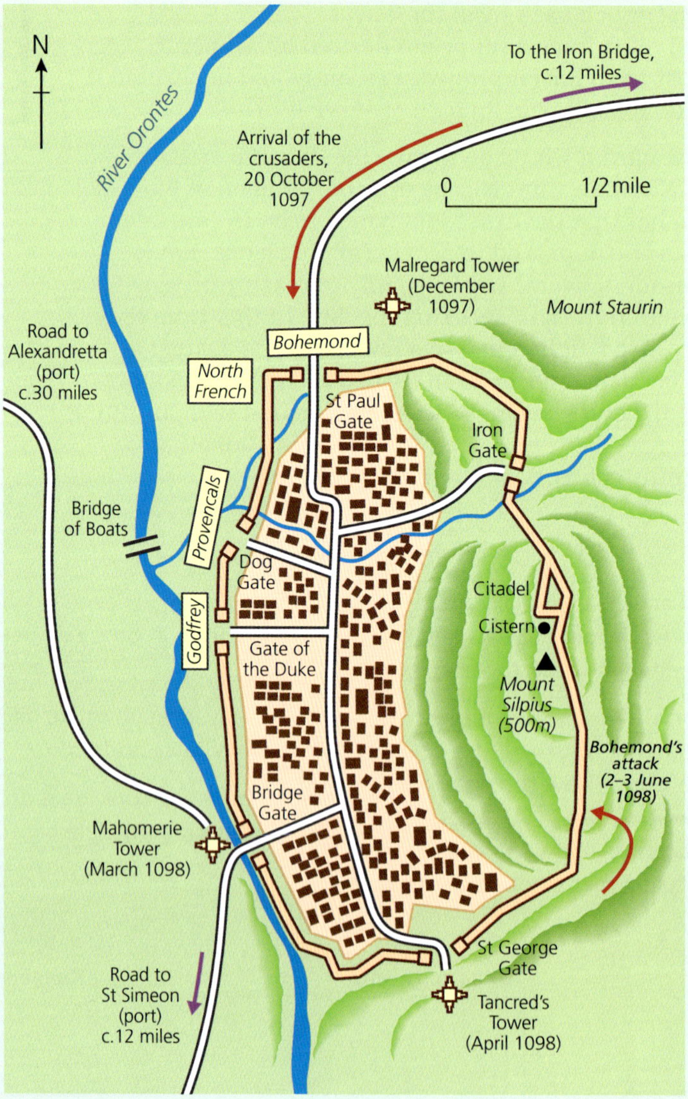

Even if the crusaders took the main city, they would then have to take the fortified citadel on the cliffs at the top of the mountains.

From the top of the mountain behind the city, the Turks could observe the crusader camp. Anyone who left the main camp, for example to forage for food, might be ambushed by Turks who had slipped out of the city.

▲ Antioch: features and events, October 1097–June 1098

Reflect

Which of the features shown here do you think was most likely to slow up the capture of Antioch?

Why did it take the crusaders so long to capture the city of Antioch?

Seeking control – November to December 1097

No siege can succeed without control of the surrounding area. In particular, the besieging army needs to be confident that it will not be attacked from behind. In this case, unknown to the crusaders, Yaghi Siyan, the Seljuk governor of Antioch, could expect little or no help from further afield. A power struggle was taking place throughout Seljuk-held lands and the rulers of different regions were competing with each other for power. Rulers of cities such as Aleppo and Damascus left Yaghi Siyan to face the crusaders alone. He sent out pleas for help but there would be no speedy response from fellow Muslim rulers across the region.

The roads to the coast

The crusaders would not be able to rely on finding food and supplies locally. They had to gain control over the roads to the Syrian ports so that Alexios could send them supplies from his island of Cyprus. The roads to the coast ran on the west bank of the River Orontes and the only crossing at Antioch was at the Bridge Gate. This was securely held by the Turks.

In October 1097, the crusaders found a rather precarious solution to this problem. They lashed lots of small boats together across the River Orontes to make a temporary bridge quite close to their camp (see map on page 64). This became a target for the Turks taking pot-shots at the crusaders as they staggered over the makeshift structure, but it did allow access to the ports.

Yaghi Siyan could see that this bridge was a lifeline for the crusaders so, in December 1097, Turkish forces rushed out from Bridge Gate and raced towards the Bridge of Boats. Raymond of Toulouse tried to defend the area but he and his men were forced to retreat over the Bridge of Boats to safety. The scene of so many men scrambling over that rickety structure was chaotic, but somehow they made it back. Although Raymond was now safe and the bridge could still be used, the Turks had captured a precious crusader flag and they regularly waved it from their walls to mock the Franks.

The roads to the north

In December, the crusaders built their own fort on the slopes of a hill that overlooked the road to the north, quite close to the city walls. It was given the name 'Malregard', which means ill-looking. It was probably made of earthworks rather than stone or timber. This protected the crusader camp from surprise Turkish raids from the garrison. It also helped to control the road to the north and allowed crusaders to forage further afield for the food they needed.

On 31 December, a foraging expedition set off along the northern road to try to bring much needed food back to the city. It was made up of a strong force of knights and foot soldiers led by Bohemond and Robert of Flanders. It stumbled on a very large Turkish army that had at last been sent by the ruler of Damascus to try to relieve Antioch. The crusaders just managed to defeat the Turks and send them south again, but the foraging expedition returned without food and the crusaders' inability to control the surrounding area meant that they faced a desperate, hungry winter.

> ## Reflect
> Which do you think mattered more to the crusaders: the road to the coast or the road to the north?

◀ Knights crossing a boat-bridge, from a fourteenth-century manuscript

Surviving winter – January to February 1098

As they struggled with the bitter cold of a Syrian winter, the crusaders faced two serious challenges.

The threat of starvation

By January 1098, while Turks inside the city walls still had plentiful supplies, the crusader army was hungry, exhausted and depressed. Armenian and Greek traders in the locality of the camp exploited the Franks' hunger by introducing massive price rises. By now, wealth and social status meant that a person got food, otherwise it was hopeless. The situation was so serious that Stephen of Blois resorted to giving his own money away to help the starving. Death through starvation was now probable rather than possible for most crusaders.

The new year brought a comet in the skies. This and a recent earthquake were seen as signs of God's displeasure. In response, Bishop Adhemar called for an extreme programme of religious activity, involving intense prayer and going without food, drink and sex for days on end: the bishop banned women from the camp. This spiritual self-denial did not seem to help. Nor did a crackdown on sins such as theft, which involved public whippings for offenders. Many crusaders deserted. In late January, Peter the Hermit and a noble, curiously called William the Carpenter, snuck away under cover of darkness. They were captured and returned by Tancred. Peter and William were too well-known to be punished, and instead they made a public promise to stay. So did all the princes.

The threat from Aleppo

In February 1098, another force of Turks, this time from Aleppo, arrived in response to Yaghi Siyan's call for help. Seven hundred knights led by Bohemond, Robert of Flanders and Stephen of Blois rode out to confront them. Raymond of Toulouse was too unwell to join them and he stayed to defend the camp.

Despite being heavily outnumbered, the crusaders went on the offensive. They attacked the force from Aleppo at night with an ambush on the road near the Iron Bridge (see map on page 63). Bohemond hid a division of cavalry back for a surprise attack, waiting for just the right moment to pounce. The *Gesta Francorum* proudly describes his success:

> Bohemond, protected on all sides by the sign of the Cross, charged the Turkish forces like a lion which has been starving for three or four days which comes out of its cave thirsting for the blood of cattle and falls upon the flocks careless of their own safety, tearing the sheep as they flee hither and thither.

By now, the princes were deploying tactics inspired by the Turks. Small, mobile cavalry units of mounted knights wove between the enemy, picking them off one by one. Eventually, the Aleppo Turks retreated.

Stalemate

By the end of February, the situation had reached stalemate. The crusaders had beaten off the Aleppo relief force and those crusaders who had managed to survive were becoming more effective warriors. Wealthy crusaders pooled their funds to support the poor and pay for defences. But there was no sign of Tatikios who had left in early February to seek more food and soldiers. The crusade was still outside Antioch's walls.

> ## Reflect
> How might the hardship of the winter have helped the crusade in the longer term?

◀ Pilgrims at prayer, from a fifteenth-century manuscript

Why did it take the crusaders so long to capture the city of Antioch?

The siege tightens – spring 1098

Early March brought some hope with the arrival of an English fleet at St Simeon. Some historians say this had been arranged by Tatikios as he had promised, but the evidence is uncertain. The food would end the winter supply crisis and the ships also brought skilled carpenters and others who were experts in making siege engines.

Bohemond and Raymond were sent with 500 knights to collect the goods and escort the engineers to the camp. On the way back, they were so laden down with food and building material that it took them three days to complete a journey that might normally take less than one.

The battle at Bridge Gate

As they approached Antioch with these English supplies, the supply convoy was ambushed by Turkish soldiers who had made their way out of the city through Bridge Gate. The *Gesta Francorum* described how these Turks used similar tactics to those used at the Battle of Dorylaeum:

> The Turks began to gnash their teeth and chatter and howl with very loud cries, wheeling round our men, throwing darts and loosing arrows … Their attack was so fierce our men began to flee over the nearest mountain … Those who could get away quickly escaped alive, and those who could not were killed.

▲ An English Heritage artist's reconstruction of an eleventh-century carpenter at work

The Turks captured the precious supplies but the knights rallied. With help from a force led by Godfrey of Bouillon, they managed to regain the goods and take them safely to their camp. Although this 'battle' of Bridge Gate was not significant in terms of numbers taking part, it did have a positive impact on the crusaders' morale, and weakened the Turkish forces in Antioch.

A firmer grip

The leaders' council decided to use the timber to build a siege tower at Bridge Gate. This would prevent similar ambushes by Turks from the city and provide safer access to the main road to St Simeon. Within a week the tower was completed. It was funded and controlled by Raymond of Toulouse.

Soon, other supplies and reinforcements arrived from Baldwin of Edessa and supply lines to Antioch were improved by establishing crusader outposts in regions around the city. Raymond of Toulouse guarded the south, Godfrey and Robert of Flanders held the north-east and Tancred occupied the east. By April 1098 the crusaders had almost encircled the city and secured the surrounding area.

Despite these minor successes, by May 1098 the crusaders were still staring at Antioch's walls.

Reflect

How does the author of the *Gesta Francorum* create such a terrifying account of the ambush?

Record

1. Finish making notes on this part of your explanation timeline (see page 63).
2. When your timeline for this section is complete, use two different colours to highlight:
   a) things that the crusaders **could control**
   b) things that the crusaders **could not control**.

Record

Start making the second section on your explanation timeline (see page 63). At the top of this section, use the heading '**The capture of Antioch, May to June 1098**'.

The capture of Antioch

In February 1098, Tatikios, who represented Emperor Alexios on the princes' council, had left Antioch to seek supplies and reinforcements. Since then supplies had arrived in March but no one was sure if these came from him. By May 1098, there was still no sign of Tatikios, Alexios or any Byzantine army of reinforcements.

Relations between the crusader princes and the Byzantine Emperor had always been strained. The oath of loyalty sworn at Constantinople was coming under increasing pressure. As doubts grew about the lordship of Alexios, so too did the simmering tensions between the crusader princes themselves.

Two rivals jostle for power

Without the presence of Alexios or even his general Tatikios, it was less clear than ever who should make the big decisions about the crusade. Two of the princes in particular jostled for power as the siege continued: Bohemond of Taranto and Raymond of Toulouse. Each could claim to be playing a vital role in the siege of Antioch, as the summaries below show.

▼ These images of Bohemond and Raymond are from cards made for collecting in nineteenth-century France

Bohemond of Taranto

Bohemond had always been a formidable figure but the extended stay at Antioch gave him the opportunity to prove that he should control the city. Daring, brave and with considerable military skill, he had led the Crusade army on dangerous foraging missions and defeated Turkish relief forces from Damascus and Aleppo in battle. He had a large number of followers, including his tenacious, brave nephew, Tancred. Between them, they had secured control of two gates: Bohemond built the Malregard Tower near the St Paul Gate in December 1097 and Tancred set up his own tower at the south end of the city by the St George Gate in April 1098.

At a princes' council at the end of May, Bohemond demanded that he should have sole control of Antioch, claiming that he had done more than anyone to tighten the crusaders' grip on the city. Even though his demand was refused, he was not going to give up easily.

Raymond of Toulouse

Raymond had considerable experience of campaigning and had a large following. He had made the strategic decision to lay siege to Antioch and had been left to defend the siege camp against repeated attacks from inside the Turkish garrison. His age brought experience, but also illness: he was often unable to support others when they rode out to deal with more distant military threats.

Raymond had the wealth to maintain his huge following. He built and funded the great siege tower called La Mahomerie by the Bridge Gate and controlled that vital area. He was the only prince to refuse Bohemond's demands at the Crusader Council in May.

Why did it take the crusaders so long to capture the city of Antioch?

The question of control

Byzantine sources show that Alexios felt that he had held his side of the bargain. He was supplying the crusaders from Cyprus through the ports along the coast. He still believed in the binding nature of the promises made by the princes, sworn in the presence of God. The question was whether the crusaders would keep those promises after months of appalling siege conditions and with no sign of his support.

Even though the crusaders were still not in the city, the question of what would happen to Antioch if the siege could be broken was often discussed. This matter was at the heart of the rivalries in the leadership.

By May, tensions between Bohemond and Raymond were at breaking point. News had reached the crusaders that a massive Turkish army was on its way to relieve the city. The whole crusade was in crisis. Bohemond had already been asking the other princes to hand Antioch over to him if and when it fell. Now, at an emergency meeting on 31 May 1098, fearing the imminent arrival of the Turkish army, the princes finally agreed to compromise on Bohemond's demands. The *Gesta Francorum* records how they said:

> if Bohemond can take this city, either by himself or by others, we will thereafter give it to him gladly, on condition that if the Emperor come to our aid and fulfil all his obligations which he promised and vowed, we will return the city to him as it is right to do.

Of course, none of this mattered if the crusaders could not find a way into the city before the Muslim army arrived. That looked to be very unlikely.

Reflect

What does the quotation from the emergency meeting of May 1098 suggest about the princes' attitude to their oaths to Alexios at this stage?

The approaching army

The Turkish relief force was led by Kerbogha, the powerful ruler of Mosul, a large and wealthy city about 300 miles east of Antioch. He had gathered an army so large that it probably outnumbered the 25,000 or so crusaders who had survived the long journey to Antioch, the battles and starvation.

Kerbogha left Mosul at the end of April and should have appeared at Antioch by mid-May. Fortunately for the crusaders, he did not. He had heard how Baldwin had become ruler of Edessa which lay close to his own route to Antioch. Fearing that Baldwin may attack him as he travelled west, Kerbogha laid siege to Edessa for three weeks. Eventually he decided that it was safe to head for Antioch without capturing Edessa first. By the time he arrived, however, the Franks had made their breakthrough and were behind Antioch's high walls: Bohemond had got his wish.

▼ A general leads his troops into battle. From a Muslim manuscript, c.1300

Treachery and trickery as Antioch falls

When the princes signed the future lordship of Antioch over to Bohemond at the emergency meeting of 31 May, they didn't all realise that Bohemond had a secret. He knew how he could take the city. His secret weapon came in the form of an Armenian armour-maker called Firuz who lived and worked inside Antioch. Historians have argued over whether Bohemond had deliberately withheld this information or whether he kept his fellow princes informed.

No one knows exactly who the mysterious figure of Firuz was, or how he first made contact with Bohemond. Anna Komnena tells us that they met by chatting over the wall of Antioch, but it is more likely that contact was made through Armenian traders. Why Firuz wanted to help the crusaders is also a mystery. Perhaps he was motivated by the riches Bohemond offered him or perhaps Yaghi Siyan had taken away his wealth. Some sources suggest that he was motivated by visions of Christ.

Whatever drove him, the most important thing about Firuz was that he guarded a remote section of the city walls on the mountain side above the St George Gate. It is clear that by mid-May Bohemond had persuaded Firuz to help the crusader army to break into the city over its walls.

▲ A twentieth-century engraving of Bohemond's knights climbing into Antioch

Why did it take the crusaders so long to capture the city of Antioch?

Here is how the *Gesta Francorum* describes the action:

> The plan was made and the date was set for the night of the 2–3 June. The men came to the ladder, which was already set up and lashed firmly to the battlements of the city. When Firuz saw that only a few of our men had come up, he was afraid, in case he should fall into the hands of the Turks, and said, 'Where is the hero Bohemond?' A soldier went back and ran as fast as he could to find him. Bohemond arrived rejoicing to the ladder. Now an amazing number of men began to climb; they went up and began to run quickly to the other towers.
>
> Meanwhile, the ladder happened to break and we were plunged into despair. There was a gate not far from us, but it was shut and some of us did not know where it was in the darkness. Yet by fumbling with our hands we found it and all made a rush at it. We broke it down.

Here is how historian Christopher Tyerman describes the crusaders' entry into Antioch in his 2006 book, *God's War*:

> Contact across the front line at Antioch was common ... Bohemond and his followers possessed a linguistic advantage in this: on the night of the agreed commando-style raid on his section of the walls, they were able to converse with Firuz in Greek. However the small force which established itself under the cover of dark on the inside included Godfrey of Bouillon and Robert of Flanders. Tancred, Count Raymond and Bishop Adhemar had also been let into the secret and were instrumental in rousing the main army to exploit the incursion the following morning.

Reflect

How useful are the following for a historian studying the crusaders' entry to Antioch:

- the extract from the *Gesta Francorum* (above left)
- the engraved interpretation by a twentieth-century artist showing crusaders climbing into Antioch (page 70)
- the interpretation by historian Christopher Tyerman (above right)?

Atrocity as Antioch is taken

Once the crusaders had breached the city walls, Christians still living within Antioch opened the city's remaining gates. The crusaders flooded in and Bohemond ordered that his banner be flown from the highest point of the city. In the early hours of 3 June 1098, Yaghi Siyan fled his city, leaving his people to face the invaders without him. He was caught and beheaded by a local peasant.

A Muslim force managed to keep hold of the citadel perched on the cliffs overlooking the city below. From their relative safety they must have witnessed the bloody massacre of the inhabitants below.

In the light of dawn, the crusaders could be seen hacking their way through the streets of Antioch, brutally killing the city's population and robbing bodies and buildings. They even killed the Christian population of Antioch, the very people they had set out to liberate.

Consequences of the massacre

News of this atrocity sent a warning to other cities in Syria about just what the crusaders were capable of. Their reputation as a ruthless, hardened fighting force would walk with them to Jerusalem. The crusaders had now taken the city, but at a terrible cost in human life. Whatever we think today about the way in which the crusaders entered the city, they now had control of Antioch itself. Strangely, however, their greatest crisis lay ahead.

Record

1. Finish making notes on this part of your explanation timeline (see page 63).
2. When your timeline for this section is complete, use two different colours to highlight:
   a) things that the crusaders **could control**
   b) things that the crusaders **could not control**.

The defeat of Kerbogha

Whatever joy or relief the crusaders may have felt as they finally captured the city and put its people to the sword, it was to be short-lived. Kerbogha's huge Muslim army from Mosul began to arrive the very next day, 4 June 1098. Anyone left in the crusader camp had to hurry into the shelter of the city. The crusaders had now become the besieged. It had taken them eight months to struggle into Antioch, only to face the prospect of dying there.

Trapped in Antioch

At first, Kerbogha gathered his forces behind the high ground of the city, trying to break in near the citadel where the remains of Antioch's Turkish garrison were stationed. Bohemond established a camp high up in Antioch, south of the citadel, and began to build a wall to protect the rest of the city just in case Kerbogha managed to break through.

Acts of extreme bravery were recorded during these difficult weeks. A knight nicknamed 'Mad Hugh' defended a tower single-handedly, breaking three spears in the process. Unfortunately, by now not all the crusaders were as determined. Kerbogha launched a particularly violent attack on the city on 10 June. It lasted for four days. For many, this was the final straw and they deserted, lowering themselves down the walls of Antioch on ropes, hoping to make a run for it. Even Stephen of Blois, officially the leader of the princes' council, fled. These deserters were nicknamed 'rope danglers'. The situation was so bad that the princes pledged to stay while Bohemond and Bishop Adhemar of Le Puy arranged for the city gates to be barricaded so that no one could escape or let the enemy in. In the days to come, however, it would be Adhemar's role as a religious leader that was to be of particular importance to the future of the crusade.

On 14 June, Kerbogha gave up on his direct attack and moved a large part of his army down onto the plains and settled into a lengthy siege, just as the crusaders had done before him. He set up a base camp on the road north of the city and waited for the siege to take effect.

It soon did. The crusaders became increasingly desperate. Shut away in Antioch, with no supplies reaching them from outside and no prospect of safely gathering more, they found themselves isolated and miserable. Chroniclers report how any food was sold at ridiculous prices and the crusaders resorted to boiling and eating leaves, thistles and roots of stinging nettles. They ate the flesh and skin of donkeys, camels, oxen and, most precious of all, their own horses. They needed a miracle.

Visions and hope

On 11 June, the day after Kerbogha's great assault began, Stephen of Valence, a priest from southern France, declared that he had recently seen a vision. Christ had come to promise him that the crusaders would receive his direct help in five days' time if they would only demonstrate their faith in him.

Raymond of Toulouse was fully convinced by these visions, but Bishop Adhemar was sceptical. Despite his reservations, he once again organised prayers, processions and self-denial by all the crusaders. These continued as Kerbogha's violent attack raged around them. Then, at about the same time, a young pilgrim called Peter Bartholomew, also from southern France, announced that he too had received a vision from God. It told him where he could find one of the holiest of all relics: the spear that had been used by a Roman soldier to pierce the side of Christ on the cross.

> **Record**
> Start making the final section of your explanation timeline (see page 63). At the top of this section use the heading **'The defeat of Kerbogha, June 1098'**.

▼ A bishop, from a fourteenth-century manuscript about the preaching of the First Crusade. It may represent Adhemar who was a close supporter of the pope and who was appointed as his representative on the crusade

Why did it take the crusaders so long to capture the city of Antioch?

The Holy Lance

Peter Bartholomew's visions told him that the Holy Lance was to be found under the floor of the church of St Peter in Antioch. He came from the same region in southern France as Raymond of Toulouse, who gave him his support.

On 14 June, the date given to Stephen of Valence as the day when Christ would give his help, the search for the Holy Lance began. Raymond of Aguilers, who was there at the time, describes the search under the floor of the church:

> We had been digging until evening when some gave up hope of unearthing the lance. In the meantime … we persuaded fresh workers to replace the weary diggers and for a time they dug furiously. But the youthful Peter Bartholomew, seeing the exhaustion of our workers, stripped his outer garments and, clad only in a shirt and barefooted, dropped into the hole. He then begged us to pray to God to return his lance to the crusaders, so as to bring strength and victory to his people.
>
> Finally, prompted by his gracious compassion, the Lord showed us his lance and I, Raymond, author of this book, kissed the point of the lance as it barely protruded from the ground. I cannot relate the happiness and rejoicing which filled Antioch.

Reflect

In this modern illustration of the moment when the Holy Lance was found, how has the artist tried to create a sense of drama and excitement?

▲ The unearthing of the Holy Lance, an illustration from a popular magazine c.1960

Faith and suspicion

The importance of relics to those on crusade was very real. Adhemar of Le Puy carried a small piece of wood, which he believed was from Christ's cross, and Raymond of Toulouse a chalice that belonged to the saint who had founded a famous monastery in his own locality. Wherever the relic went, so did the spiritual presence of the saint, meaning that people from all parts of society believed that saints could directly intervene to help and support those who had the relic. And now, it seemed, God had given the crusade a relic that was associated with Christ himself.

Most chroniclers report the discovery of the lance (or its metal tip, at least) as a miraculous fact. One or two sources suggest that the 'lance' had been planted by people loyal to Raymond of Toulouse. This theory argued that by being proved right for trusting Peter Bartholomew, Raymond would regain his authority in the crusade leadership after Bohemond's success. All the chroniclers, however, accept that the discovery of the lance provided them with the conviction they needed to take on Kerbogha and his huge army.

Even if modern historians discount the idea that the crusaders had miraculously found the actual Holy Lance, they too accept that this incident changed the crusade: it re-awakened in the mass of the crusaders a sense that they were doing God's work and that his holy will would be done.

The next two pages investigate several sources about the lance and what historians have said about it. The story of the First Crusade continues on page 76.

Making sense of the story of the Holy Lance

Modern historians have to consider original sources from the time they are studying. They also research the writings of others before they decide what their own interpretation of events should be. Here is a case study about the Holy Lance.

What the sources say about the discovery of the Holy Lance

The image below is taken from an English manuscript that was made in the middle of the eleventh century. Although it was made about 50 years before the First Crusade, it reminds us that the story of Christ's death was constantly being retold to Christians in the west. The two figures standing on either side of Christ on the cross are Roman soldiers. Just as in the Bible accounts, one has offered Christ a drink on a sponge at the end of a stick. The other is piercing Christ in the side with a spear. He did this to check that Jesus had died before the body was taken down.

The following extracts are from the writings of the crusaders:

Gesta Francorum, c.1103
And so, that man found the lance, and they all took it up with great joy and dread, and throughout the city there was boundless rejoicing. From that hour we decided on a plan of attack, and all our leaders held a council and arranged to send a messenger to Christ's enemies the Turks, asking them why they have been so rash as to enter the land which belongs to the Christians and to us.

Raymond of Aguilers, c.1105
Then the mighty hand of God so revealed itself that he strengthened all hearts with a hope and faith so that each Christian felt that he had won a victory. Their zest for combat returned as they encouraged one another, and the crowd paralysed by fear and poverty only a few days before, now questioned any delay of battle. Consequently, the chieftains set the battle date, and then sent Peter the Hermit to Kerbogha, with orders that he abandon the siege of Antioch.

An extract from a letter from the crusader princes to Urban II, September 1098
We were so comforted and strengthened by [the Lance's] discovery and by so many other divine revelations that some of us who had been discouraged and fearful beforehand, then became courageous and resolute to fight, encouraging each other.

> ## Reflect
> What can these sources tell us about the effects of the discovery of the Holy Lance?

▲ The crucifixion of Christ, from a Bible made in Winchester, England, c.1050

Why did it take the crusaders so long to capture the city of Antioch?

What later medieval chroniclers and a modern historian say about the discovery of the Holy Lance

Matthew of Edessa, an Armenian Christian chronicler, c.1130
Kerbogha's army arrived [at Antioch]. Being seven times larger than the Frankish force, their troops violently besieged and harassed it. Then the Franks became threatened with a famine, because provisions in the city had long become exhausted. More and more hard-pressed, they resolved to obtain from Kerbogha a promise of amnesty [safety] on condition that they deliver the city into his hands and return to their own country.

Ralph of Caen, a chronicler who served the Normans during the Second Crusade, c.1135. Here he describes his version of how the lance head was found.
Peter had secreted the iron point from an Arab spear that he had found by chance. It was rough, old and worn and dissimilar in form and size to what we use. He felt that because of the novel shape of the spearhead, people would believe his story.

Peter therefore seized the moment for his deception. Picking up a hoe, he jumped into the ditch and turned towards a corner. While digging he said, 'here it is, here lies that for which we have been searching ...'. Then, adding more and more blows, he struck the lance which he had fraudulently placed in the ditch. The trickery was aided by the shadow.

An Arab chronicler, Ibn al-Athir, writing c.1200. His work was based on Muslim accounts from the time of the crusade.
After taking Antioch, the Franks stayed there for twelve days without food. The wealthy ate their horses and the poor ate carrion and leaves from the trees. Their leaders, faced with this situation, wrote to Kerbogha to ask for safe conduct through his territory, but he refused, saying: 'You will have to fight your way out'.

Among the Franks was Bohemond, their commander-in-chief, but there was also a cunning monk who assured them that a lance of the Messiah, peace be upon him, was buried in the cathedral. He told them: 'If you find it, you will be victorious; otherwise it means certain death'. He had earlier buried a lance in the soil of the cathedral and erased all his tracks. He ordered the Franks to fast and make penance for three days. On the fourth day he had them enter the building with workers who dug everywhere and found the lance. The monk then cried out, 'Rejoice, for victory is certain!'

Thomas Asbridge, historian and author of *The First Crusade: A New History*, 2004
While the discovery of the Holy Lance certainly bolstered Frankish morale, it was not enough to convince them to go immediately into battle against such terrible odds. This would mean that the unearthing of the relic was not the key turning point in the second siege of Antioch, much less a watershed in the fortunes of the Crusaders.

Blind, ecstatic faith did not send the crusaders running into battle. Instead, with all other options exhausted, trapped in an intolerable predicament, they decided to place their trust in their God and risk everything in one last ditch effort.

▲ The so-called blade of the Holy Lance that is now kept in a Vienna museum. Several others exist at other sites. The gold band carries an inscription claiming that a nail used at Christ's crucifixion is held behind it

Reflect
Most historians have argued that the discovery of the lance so raised the morale of the crusaders that they were willing and able to challenge Kerbogha in battle against all the odds.

1. How does Thomas Asbridge (left) reject that conventional view?
2. Which of the sources and interpretations on pages 74–75 do you think have most influenced the thinking of Thomas Asbridge?

Into battle

The discovery of the lance certainly raised morale among the masses of the crusaders, but the leaders did not rush them straight out into battle against Kerbogha. Bishop Adhemar, who had strong doubts about the lance, could see that it might at least strengthen people's faith. Once again he arranged times of public prayer and fasting. This also allowed time to see if Emperor Alexios would appear at the last minute with a Byzantine army. In fact, Stephen of Blois, who had deserted in early June, had met Alexios in Asia Minor about ten days later. He told the emperor that all was lost at Antioch and that any attempt to help the crusaders would only lead to the loss of more men. No help was on its way.

On 27 June, with food of any sort almost completely exhausted, the leaders agreed to send Peter the Hermit to Kerbogha's camp a few miles away near the Iron Bridge. This may have been a last-ditch attempt to agree a truce and maybe to spy on the Turks as well. Either way it became clear that there would have to be a battle. The last hours in Antioch were spent giving every last scrap of food to any remaining horses.

The Battle of Antioch

On 28 June 1098, the crusaders emerged from the city. Although a much reduced force, these survivors were battle-hardened and were united under the skilful leadership of Bohemond. His battle plan was risky but inspired. The crusader army would leave the city via the Bridge Gate and take on the thinly spread band of Muslim troops outside the city walls. If they could break that line, they would head north to confront Kerbogha's main force near its camp.

The archers went first to distract the first line of Muslim forces. The infantry followed, protected at the rear by whatever mounted cavalry remained. Bohemond cleverly kept a large group in reserve to plug any gaps in the line.

A black flag, fluttering from the Turkish citadel of Antioch, alerted Kerbogha to the attack. Rather than rush to help his men near the city, he decided it would be better to wait until the crusaders had moved further away from Antioch where they would be more exposed. In the event, Kerbogha did not act quickly enough to crush the crusaders as they left the city gate, nor take the time to set up his own army in a strong position near his camp. Instead, he advanced at the worst moment and arrived at Antioch just as the tide was turning against him.

▼ Franks and Turks fighting at the Battle of Antioch, from a manuscript c.1200

Why did it take the crusaders so long to capture the city of Antioch?

Victory and defeat

During the battle, most crusaders engaged the Turks on foot in hand-to-hand combat, although illustrations, like this one (right), made much later in the Middle Ages, show well-equipped knights in armour riding strong, healthy horses into the ranks of the enemy. In this particular image, Bishop Adhemar is shown on horseback, in chain mail and wearing his bishop's mitre. He carries the Holy Lance (now fitted onto a wooden shaft).

The Muslim forces were unable to break the crusaders' determination and began to panic. Many fled the battlefield, running straight into Kerbogha and his reinforcements. With their formation broken, chaos followed. Had Kerbogha been able to unite his troops, he might have won the battle. Instead, simmering tensions within the Muslim force erupted, fracturing any hope of a unified response. Kerbogha's only option was to turn his ragged army around and retreat to Mosul. The crusaders joyfully looted his camp for food and riches, killing anyone they found. Within hours the Turkish garrison in Antioch's citadel had also surrendered.

The crusaders were soon sharing stories of miraculous help that had turned the battle in their favour: some said that Kerbogha himself had been paralysed when his eyes fell on the Holy Lance carried by Adhemar; others reported that a host of dead Christian saints all dressed in pure white had appeared from the mountains to join the battle. It is certainly true that the priests who were part of the crusader force, marched, singing and praying, into battle alongside the soldiers. The crusaders saw the victory as another blessing from God but, one way or another, they had finally gained complete control of the city that they had been struggling to capture for over eight months. They had somehow passed their 'greatest test'.

▲ The Battle of Antioch, from a history of the crusades written by William of Tyre, c.1180. William was born in Jerusalem c.1130 and lived there his whole life. Although he wrote his account c.1180, this image appeared in a version of his book that was made about 70 years later

Reflect

The image above shows a scene from the Battle of Antioch in 1098. It was made long after the time of the crusade and fails to match evidence from the time about what actually happened at the Battle of Antioch. What use, if any, does it have for historians studying the crusade?

Record

1. Finish making notes on this part of your explanation timeline (see page 63).
2. When your timeline for this section is complete, use two different colours to highlight:
    a) things that the crusaders **could control**
    b) things that the crusaders **could not control**.

Review

Use your explanation timeline to write an essay that answers the following question:

How far do you agree with historian Christopher Tyerman that 'the fall of Antioch reflected the growing self-discipline and tenacity of the crusaders'?

CLOSER LOOK 4

The Byzantine–crusader relationship: explaining the behaviour of Tatikios

One of the more intriguing characters in the story of the First Crusade is Tatikios, the Byzantine general and adviser who travelled with the crusaders across Asia Minor and fought alongside them as far as Antioch. Taking a closer look at his life and his role in the crusade helps us to understand the difference between the Byzantines and the western Christians and how their relationship developed as time went by.

The emperor's friend and servant

Surprisingly, this most loyal of Byzantines was almost certainly a Turk. He is often called a 'Saracen' in Byzantine sources. He had been captured as a very young man and became a slave in the household of Alexios's father, who was then the emperor. He became close friends with Alexios who was probably of a similar age.

The two men fought alongside each other as soldiers in the Byzantine army. This may have been when Tatikios suffered the grim facial injury that (according to some accounts) meant that he wore a false nose made of gold.

When Alexios became emperor in 1081, Tatikios became a trusted adviser and general, riding around the empire with Alexios, rather like the earlier emperor shown on the right with his own 'right-hand man' and his bodyguard. Tatikios went on to command Byzantine armies in wars around the empire, fighting Normans, Turks and Peshnegs for his master.

From 1097, Tatikios became Alexios's representative with the First Crusade as it crossed Asia Minor. He probably chose its route and may have sent Baldwin to Cilicia to ensure that the crusaders took the key towns to make certain that Alexios would regain from the Turks the lands that he so badly wanted. He may even have arranged for Baldwin to become the new ruler of Edessa, ensuring that Alexios had a strong and grateful servant in that important region.

But it was at Antioch, in the bitter winter of 1097–98, that the crusaders lost trust in Tatikios and Alexios. They began to wonder whether the Byzantine emperor was really committed to taking Jerusalem now that the lands in Asia Minor had been restored to him. When Tatikios left the crusaders suffering and claimed he was going to find supplies and reinforcements, they were doubtful. When no supplies came for many weeks, they became convinced that he and Alexios had betrayed them.

His disappearance caused arguments between crusaders at the time and was recorded differently by chroniclers in the east and the west. It still causes debate among historians today.

▲ A ninth-century Byzantine emperor with his advisers and bodyguard. From an eleventh-century Greek manuscript

Reflect

Page 79 shows how two historians have interpreted the behaviour of Tatikios at Antioch very differently. Read both interpretations and decide which one you find more convincing.

The Byzantine–crusader relationship: explaining the behaviour of Tatikios

The historians' debate

In his book *The First Crusade: A New History* (2004), Thomas Asbridge summarises the more traditional view of the actions of Tatikios:

> Since leaving Constantinople the Franks had been accompanied by the Greek guide and adviser, Tatikios. At the end of January, he announced his intention to travel back into Asia Minor in search of supplies and reinforcements for the siege. The crusaders had, since their arrival at Antioch, been expecting to be reinforced by the Byzantine emperor Alexios. At the time, Tatikios' proposal was probably accepted, his promise believed. Apparently, he even left all his possessions behind in camp as evidence of his determination to return. He and his men duly set off but he never returned to the siege of Antioch. This betrayal shocked the Franks, and writing with the benefit of hindsight, most crusaders' sources were deeply critical of the Greek guide's conduct.

▲ Historian Thomas Asbridge

More recently, Peter Frankopan has put forward a different interpretation of Tatikios's actions. His work emphasises the importance of the Byzantine role in the First Crusade, from its origins and purpose to its outcome at Jerusalem. In his book, *The First Crusade: The Call from the East* (2012), he describes how western chroniclers accused Tatikios (and Alexios) of abandoning the crusaders to fend for themselves at Antioch. He then argues:

> These judgements were unjustified. On 4 March 1098, a few weeks after Tatikios had left, a fleet arrived at St. Simeon's port bringing essential foodstuffs, provisions, reinforcements and materials to use against Antioch's formidable defences. Alexios had established a garrison at Laodikeia [a port further south on the Syrian coast] and it was presumably these men who now brought emergency supplies to Antioch. Tatikios had delivered what he had promised.
>
> The reason why this was not acknowledged at the time by the crusaders and their chroniclers was that misgivings had already started to grow about the Byzantine role in the expedition ... [The] western force began to question not only whether the Byzantines had lost faith in the operation, but also why the city was being besieged in the first place, at such heavy cost to westerners ... Why not simply advance to Jerusalem and leave Antioch aside?
>
> The oaths that the emperor had insisted on were proving to be highly effective [and he] evidently felt comfortable enough to think that it was not necessary to dispatch Tatikios back to the western camp to ensure that the obligations remained intact ... On more than one occasion, Bohemond had intervened on Alexios' behalf. If the emperor thought Bohemond would continue to represent him, he was wrong.

▲ Historian Peter Frankopan

5 To the Holy City

How did the crusaders establish the Kingdom of Jerusalem?

For the crusaders, the victory at Antioch in August 1098 was a great achievement, but this did not stop the squabbling between the crusade's leaders. Bohemond was sure that he was the rightful ruler of Antioch. Raymond of Toulouse argued that the city should be given to Alexios I although he probably wanted it for himself. The two men were bitterly divided. To make matters worse, Bishop Adhemar, who had provided spiritual leadership to the crusade, died on 1 August 1098. During the autumn of 1098, the First Crusade ground to a halt.

In January 1099, pressure from ordinary crusaders, who were determined to reach Jerusalem, broke the stalemate. During the spring and summer of 1099, the crusading army journeyed south. At the beginning of June, around 14,000 crusaders finally arrived at the walls of Jerusalem. On 14 July, they captured the Holy City. The bloodshed which followed was deeply disturbing, even by the standards of medieval warfare.

This image, from a fourteenth-century biography of Godfrey of Bouillon, shows the crusaders attaching Jerusalem in July 1099. It includes a mysterious knight who, according to some chronicle accounts, appeared on the Mount of Olives to direct the crusaders' attack.

▼ The capture of Jerusalem in 1099, from a fourteenth-century biography of Godfrey of Bouillon

How did the crusaders establish the Kingdom of Jerusalem?

Having gained control of Jerusalem, the crusaders elected a ruler. They chose the man who had played such an important part in the success of the First Crusade, Godfrey of Bouillon. The picture on page 80 shows Geoffrey wearing a crown, but the picture distorts history. Godfrey agreed to rule the new Christian kingdom, but he declined the title of 'King of Jerusalem' believing that only Christ could hold that title.

In 1837, the Italian artist Federico de Madrazo was asked to produce a painting for the Palace of Versailles in Paris. He chose to paint this scene in the Church of the Holy Sepulchre when Godfrey of Bouillon became ruler of the Kingdom of Jerusalem.

> **Reflect**
>
> How did the artist portray Godfrey of Bouillon as a popular and pious crusader who was reluctant to take the title 'King of Jerusalem'?

▶ *The election of Godfrey of Bouillon as the King of Jerusalem on 23 July 1099.* A painting by the Italian artist Federico de Madrazo for the Palace of Versailles, Paris, 1837

The Enquiry

This enquiry focuses on the events before and after Godfrey of Bouillon became ruler of the new Kingdom of Jerusalem on 23 July 1099. You will find out about the three final stages of the First Crusade:

1. The crusaders' long and difficult journey from Antioch to Jerusalem.
2. The capture of Jerusalem in July 1099 and the massacre of Muslims and Jews in the city.
3. The creation of the Kingdom of Jerusalem in the year before Godfrey of Bouillon's death in July 1100.

In order to explain how the crusaders were able to establish the Kingdom of Jerusalem, you will produce two sets of small cards for each of the stages. Your cards will explain:

a) the things which **helped** the crusaders
b) the things which **hindered** the crusaders.

At the end of the enquiry you will use your cards to challenge an interpretation of how the crusaders established the Kingdom of Jerusalem in the two years between July 1098 and July 1100.

To Jerusalem ... but slowly

By July 1098, the crusaders had secured Antioch and were now only a three-week march from Jerusalem. In fact, it would take them over a year to reach the Holy City. The siege at Antioch had severely weakened the crusader force. Many crusaders had died in the assault. Those who remained suffered from hunger and thirst in the heat of the Syrian summer. Disease deepened their suffering still further. In August, the pope's representative, Adhemar of Le Puy, died. Without his papal authority, the spiritual force of the crusade was weakened and there was no one to keep the individual ambitions of the crusader princes in check.

▼ The four leaders of the First Crusade: Godfrey of Bouillon, Raymond of Toulouse, Bohemond of Taranto and Tancred of Hauteville. An 1881 engraving based on a drawing by the French painter Alphonse de Neuville

Disputes and delays

This nineteenth-century engraving (left) shows the leaders of the First Crusade in the autumn of 1098. Godfrey of Bouillon is pointing the way to Jerusalem and the other leaders seem to be following. Raymond of Aguilers makes it clear that the reality was very different:

> **From Raymond of Aguilers's *History of the Franks who captured Jerusalem*, c.1101**
>
> Arguments worried leaders and undermined relationships – only a few avoided disputes with their allies. Idle and rich, the crusaders, contrary to God's commands, postponed the journey until the 1 November. If the Franks had advanced, not one city between Antioch and Jerusalem would have thrown one rock at them, as the Saracen cities were so terrified after the defeat of Kerbogha.

> ### Reflect
> Why was Raymond so frustrated by the crusaders' delay?

Throughout the autumn of 1098 arguments raged between Raymond and Bohemond over control of Antioch. Both crusader princes had strong positions: Raymond held the access routes to the sea via the Bridge Gate, and Bohemond, the citadel. Each stubbornly refused to give up their advantage.

A major area of dispute was whether the crusaders should keep their promise to Alexios that any cities conquered by the crusaders should be returned to Byzantine rule. Raymond wanted to maintain the oath while Bohemond argued that Alexios's absence meant that their promise was broken. The crusaders decided to wait to see if Alexios would come to stake his claim in person, but the Byzantine emperor remained in Constantinople, fearing a revolution if he left.

The unity of the crusade unravelled further as ties of loyalty broke down and knights began to shift their allegiance according to who might reward them best. On 1 November, the date set for leaving Antioch, the leadership of the crusade was still in crisis. It seemed that no one could provide the crusade with the leadership it so desperately needed.

How did the crusaders establish the Kingdom of Jerusalem?

Contenders for leadership

Three men were the main rivals for leadership of the crusade by November 1098.

Bohemond of Taranto

Bohemond had proved himself to be an extremely capable and strong military leader. He had fought his way through a series of difficult military situations, including leading the crusade into battle against Kerbogha. He negotiated treaties with Italian merchants from Venice and Genoa, maintaining regular supplies to the crusaders at Antioch.

Bohemond secured the crusader position by controlling the most direct route from Asia Minor to northern Syria, preventing Byzantine forces taking back control of Antioch. This focus on the security of the immediate area suggests that Bohemond's energies and ambitions were with Antioch rather than Jerusalem by summer 1098.

▲ Bohemond of Taranto

> **Reflect**
>
> Which crusader prince do you think has the strongest claim to be leader of the First Crusade?

Godfrey of Bouillon

Godfrey of Bouillon's position was increasingly strong. He had the support of his younger brother, Baldwin, who had claimed the territory of Edessa. Godfrey had become very wealthy by securing towns for Baldwin near Edessa. He used this wealth to attract new followers.

Godfrey was also increasingly seen as a natural leader by local Muslim rulers. He successfully assisted a local ruler, Omar of Azaz, to increase his power. Raymond and Bohemond rushed from Antioch to support Omar, but they were too late to take any glory. As far as Omar was concerned, it was Godfrey who was now the leader of the Franks.

▲ Godfrey of Bouillon

> **Reflect**
>
> These images of the three leaders of the First Crusade are from nineteenth-century trading cards. People collected these cards and swapped them with their friends. What impression do they give of the leaders?

Raymond of Toulouse

Raymond was one of the most experienced crusader princes. He was older, approaching 60, and had a large number of followers from southern France. After the fall of Antioch, he was one of the richest leaders and used his wealth to secure more followers. He was also closely associated with the Holy Lance, seen as the key to the victory over Kerbogha. As the popularity of the Holy Lance grew, so did his support.

Despite these advantages, Raymond was not always in the best of health. Frequent illness meant that he could not always take the lead in military situations.

▲ Raymond of Toulouse

> **Record**
>
> Make some explanation cards to show what hindered the crusaders from leaving Antioch during the autumn of 1098.

The journey to Jerusalem

By mid-November no clear leader had emerged and it looked like the crusaders would have to endure another cold Syrian winter in Antioch. But they did not. The map below and the account opposite and on page 85 explain how the crusaders made the journey from Antioch to Jerusalem between November 1098 and June 1099.

> ### Reflect
> Use the map and the account to decide what helped and hindered the crusaders on their journey to Jerusalem.

▼ The route of the crusaders from Antioch to Jerusalem

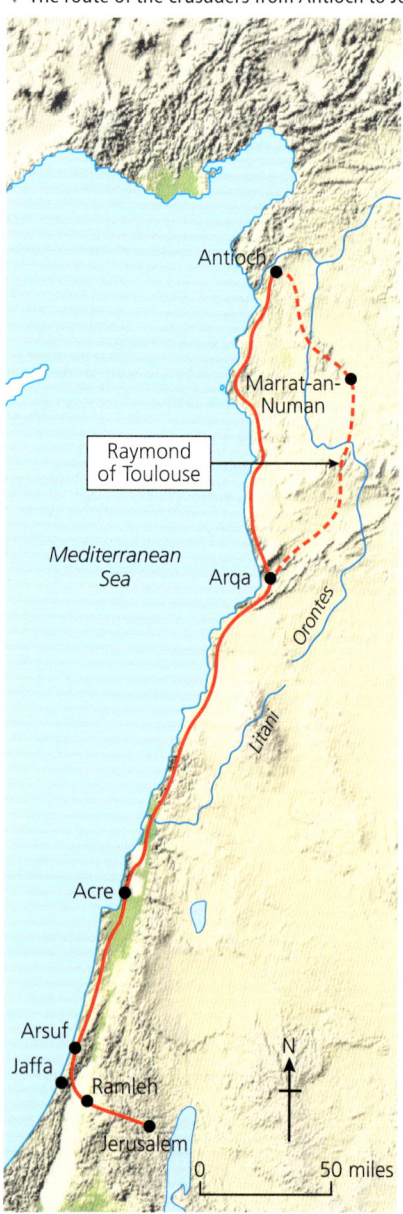

The crusaders' journey from Antioch to Jerusalem, November 1098–July 1099

November 1098

Raymond decided that the only way that he could make Bohemond hand over Antioch was to take the valley to the south. If he controlled the valley's strategic city, Marrat-an-Numan, he would be able to disrupt Bohemond's supply lines. On 23 November, Raymond led his troops south to attack the city. Godfrey of Bouillon and Robert of Flanders stayed at Antioch but Bohemond followed Raymond to Marrat so that he could keep some control over the area if it fell to Raymond. Raymond's plan had made their rivalry even more intense.

December 1098

Marrat's high walls meant that the city was very well defended. The crusaders filled in sections of the dry moat and tunnelled under the walls. They foraged for local timber and spent ten days constructing a siege tower. The full-scale attack was launched on 11 December. A section of the city walls was broken and the crusaders stormed into the city. That night was one of terror for Marrat's population. The crusaders plundered the city and murdered many inhabitants.

Worse was yet to come for the inhabitants of Marrat. At daybreak on 12 December the crusader knights realised that the poorer crusaders had beaten them to the best booty. The knights desperately tried to seize whatever was left, murdering thousands of Marrat's population as they stole their riches. The author of the *Gesta Francorum* recorded:

> Our men all entered the city, and each seized his own share of whatever goods he found in houses or cellars, and when it was dawn they killed everyone, man and woman, whom they met in any place whatsoever. No corner of the town was clear of Saracen corpses, and one could scarcely go about the streets except by treading on their dead bodies.

January 1099

There was still no unified leadership and little prospect that the crusade would head for Jerusalem. With no clear direction, discipline disintegrated. In the bitter winter months, supply lines to Marrat were broken and some starving crusaders even turned to cannibalism, eating the flesh of slaughtered Muslims. This horrified all who heard of it, both Christian and Muslim. In their desperation, poor crusaders found a way to force Raymond to head for Jerusalem: they began to tear down Marrat's walls in protest. They wanted to fulfill their crusader oath by pressing on to Jerusalem, liberating the city and returning home. On 13 January, Raymond accepted that he must give up on building power in Syria and finally led his crusaders south towards Jerusalem.

How did the crusaders establish the Kingdom of Jerusalem?

February 1099
As Raymond's crusader force moved through Syria and into Palestine, many cities allowed it to pass unchallenged. They had heard what had happened at Marrat and feared the crusaders' ferocity. Besides, some Muslim leaders were prepared to negotiate with the crusaders in order to undermine the power of the Seljuks.

Raymond decided to follow a coastal route to Jerusalem as he knew that supplies from trading ships in the Mediterranean would help the crusade. He knew that his force of fewer than 5000 was too small to take Jerusalem by itself and hoped the other crusaders would soon join him.

While he waited, he began a siege of the nearby town of Arqa. It was a terrible decision that wasted time and resources. The siege lasted until mid-May when the crusaders left for Jerusalem without capturing the town.

March 1099
Towards the end of March, the crusading forces of Godfrey of Bouillon and Robert of Flanders finally joined Raymond of Toulouse at Arqa. Even though Bohemond remained at Antioch, the crusading army was now much stronger, but the siege continued and the relationship between the leaders of the crusade was tense.

April 1099
Ever since the discovery of the Holy Lance by Peter Bartholomew at Antioch, some crusaders had accused him of fraud. Peter was challenged to an ordeal by fire and he died of his wounds after walking over burning coals. Raymond's leadership had depended on the cult of the Holy Lance and he now began to lose authority.

Around 10 April, Byzantine ambassadors arrived at Arqa. They were furious that Bohemond was still refusing to return Antioch to the Byzantine emperor. The ambassadors insisted that the princes wait for Alexios until 24 June. Raymond was prepared to wait, but most of the crusaders did not trust Alexios. Raymond's authority was further weakened. It was Godfrey of Bouillon who now emerged as the strongest force in the crusade.

May 1099
On 16 May, the crusaders left Arqa unconquered and headed for Jerusalem with great speed. They wanted to give the Fatimid forces defending the Holy City as little time as possible to organise their defence. The crusaders continued south and met little resistance from the coastal towns. On 30 May, they marched past Arsuf and hurried inland for Jerusalem.

June 1099
On 3 June, the crusaders reached the town of Ramleh which they found abandoned. The Fatimid forces defending the town had fled. Fatimid weakness in defending Palestine meant that the crusade continued unchallenged. Three days later, the crusaders loaded up grain supplies found at Ramleh and set off on the final leg of their journey. Some walked the last few miles barefoot as pilgrims. It was this deep religious motivation that had sustained them throughout their long journey from Antioch. On 7 June, when the crusaders saw the Holy City, many of them wept. Their journey was at an end. But a terrible battle was about to begin.

▲ In this nineteenth-century engraving, the artist Gustav Doré imagines the moment when the crusaders first set eyes on Jerusalem in June 1099. The holy city shines in the distance as the crusaders give thanks for reaching their destination

Record

Make some more explanation cards to show what helped and what hindered the crusaders on their journey to Jerusalem.

The capture of Jerusalem

On 7 June 1099, around a third of the crusaders who had left Europe three years earlier now stood before the walls of Jerusalem. They made their first attack on 13 June but the city's powerful defences held firm. The crusaders spent the next three weeks planning another full-scale assault. They had to take into account all the factors shown in this diagram:

▶ This bird's eye view of Jerusalem from the south-east was made c.1800. Although the city's buildings had changed since 1099, the landscape and overall shape was largely unchanged

In the north

The disputes between the leaders of the crusade did not disappear at Jerusalem. The army divided into two. The larger group included Godfrey of Bouillon, Robert of Flanders and Tancred of Hauteville. It was positioned to the north between the Quadrangular Tower and St Stephen's Gate.

In the south

Raymond of Toulouse set up camp to the south near Zion Gate. His troops would be attacking a heavily defended area of the city walls protected by a dry moat.

Inside the city

Iftikar ad-Daulah, commander of the Fatimid garrison at Jerusalem, prepared well for the attack. He ordered his troops to repair the walls, and to hang bales of straw over them to cushion the blows from crusader catapults. The Fatimids built up stores of food and had access to a constant supply of clean water from Jerusalem's underground cisterns. They also forced many eastern Christians to leave the city.

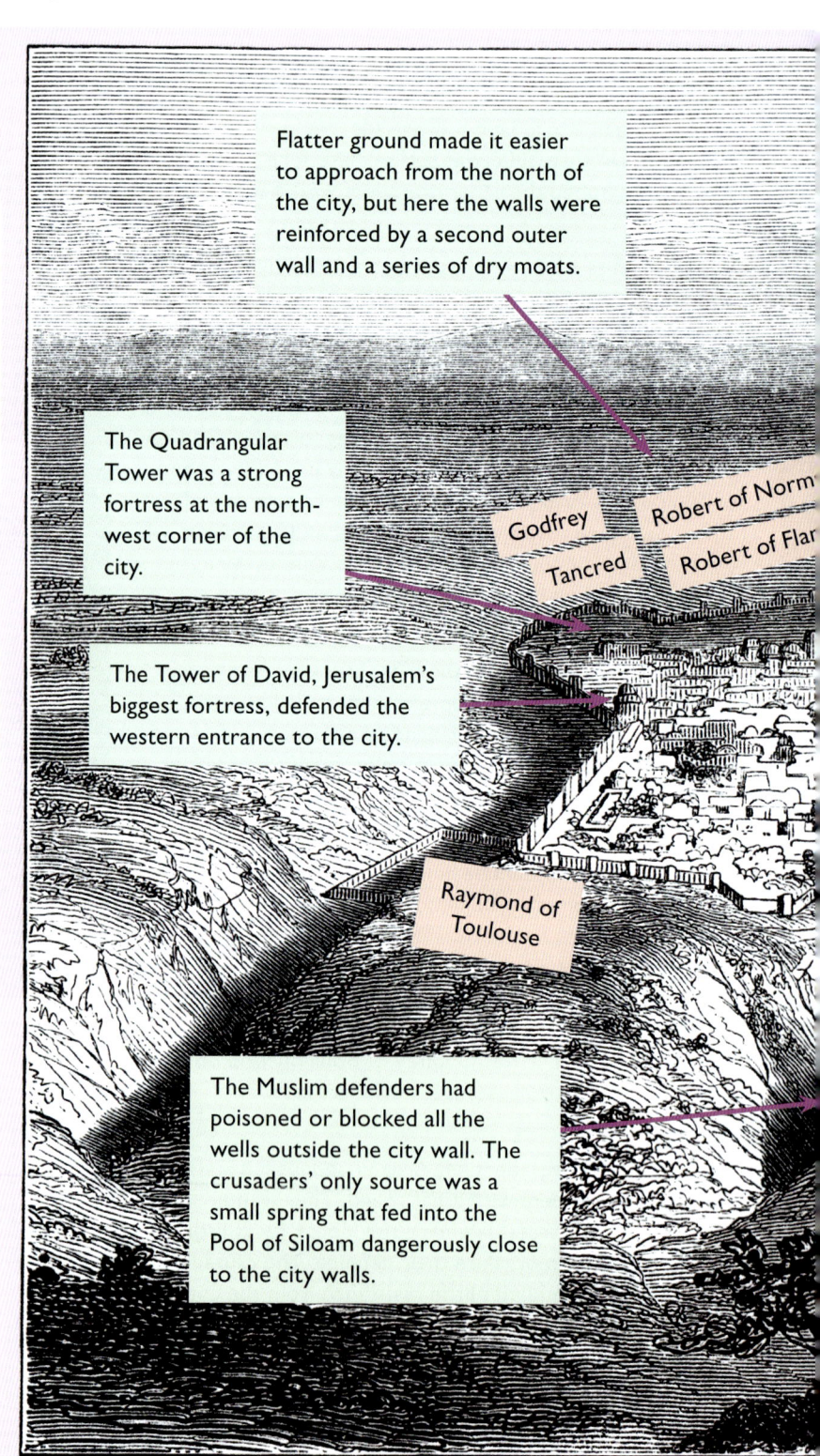

Flatter ground made it easier to approach from the north of the city, but here the walls were reinforced by a second outer wall and a series of dry moats.

The Quadrangular Tower was a strong fortress at the north-west corner of the city.

Godfrey
Tancred
Robert of Norm
Robert of Flar

The Tower of David, Jerusalem's biggest fortress, defended the western entrance to the city.

Raymond of Toulouse

The Muslim defenders had poisoned or blocked all the wells outside the city wall. The crusaders' only source was a small spring that fed into the Pool of Siloam dangerously close to the city walls.

How did the crusaders establish the Kingdom of Jerusalem?

> **Reflect**
>
> What helped and what hindered the crusaders in their attack on Jerusalem?

Position of St Stephen's Gate. The city had five major gates. Each one was well fortified.

Steep valleys made it difficult to approach the walls in the east, south and west.

Jerusalem's stone walls were fifteen metres high and three metres thick.

Supplies

On 17 June, six Genoese ships carrying vital supplies landed at Jaffa (see map on page 84). They brought timber, axes, hammers, nails and ropes. Several of the Genoese sailors were skilled carpenters. A group of crusaders travelled to Jaffa. On the way they were attacked by a Fatimid patrol, but managed to reach the port. The crusaders rescued the supplies and sailors from the ships before the Fatimids destroyed the fleet.

Siege weapons

The crusaders knew that they would have to build huge siege towers to breach Jerusalem's walls. But they faced the problem that the region around Jerusalem had few trees. Local Christians helped them to find nearby woodlands so that two huge siege towers could be built. Genoese sailors also carried timbers from their own ships to build these towers. Each one was three storeys tall and was built on a wheeled platform so that it could be moved against the walls at the right moment. The siege engines were protected from fire and arrows by thick animal skins. In addition to the two siege towers, the crusaders built scaling ladders, catapults and a battering ram with a heavy iron tip.

Spiritual preparation

Once their plan of attack had been formed, the crusaders made their spiritual preparation: on 8 July they processed barefoot around the city walls, carrying relics, and praying to God for courage.

By 14 July they were ready for action.

The final assault: July 1099

At dawn on 14 July, the crusaders began their assault on Jerusalem. During the night, Godfrey's men had broken down their siege tower at the Quadrangular Tower and had rebuilt it at the weakest spot in the walls, just east of St Stephen's Gate. It was a clever strategy that required massive effort. On the morning of 14 July, the crusaders' priority was to break down the outer curtain with their battering ram. For hours, Fatimid fire, boulders and arrows rained down on them, but by the end of the day Godfrey's men had managed to make a gap in the outer walls.

To the south, faced with fierce fire from the Fatimids' mangonels, Raymond of Toulouse's men had been less successful. Overall, the crusaders had made some progress, but, as darkness fell, crusaders in both camps must have feared what the following day would bring.

15 July 1099

At first light on 15 July, the assault began again. To the south, Raymond's forces once again faced ferocious attack. When they pushed their siege tower to the walls, the Fatimids bombarded it with rocks and fire. The crusaders were horrified to see their siege tower catch fire and collapse.

▶ An illustration of the conquest of Jerusalem in July 1099, from a fourteenth-century edition of William of Tyre's *History of the Kingdom of Jerusalem*, written c.1184

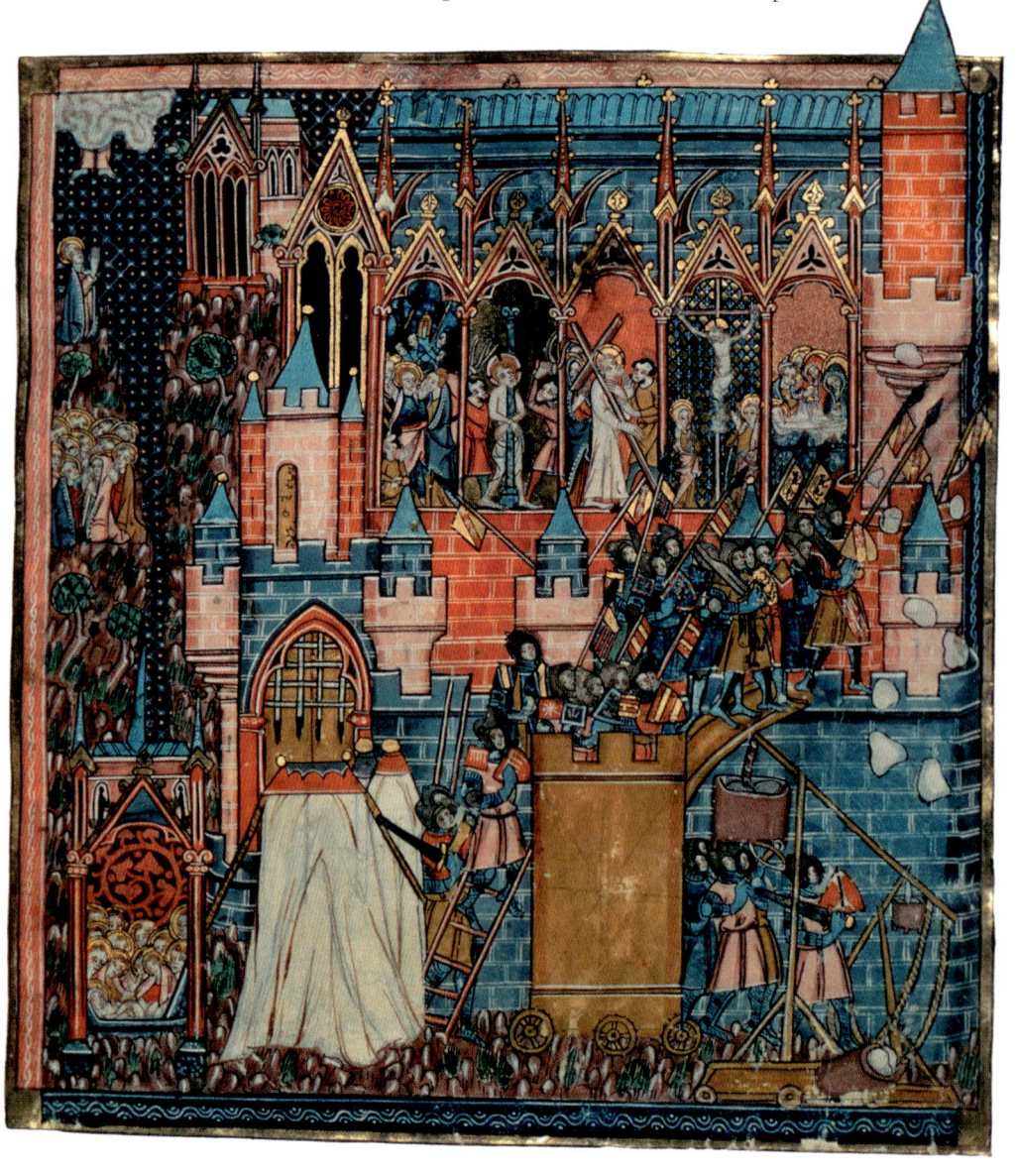

How did the crusaders establish the Kingdom of Jerusalem?

It was in the north that the assault succeeded. Godfrey climbed to the top of his siege tower to direct its dangerous journey to the city walls. As the huge siege tower approached the walls, he nearly died when a stone missile hit the head of the person next to him, killing the crusader instantly. When the tower was against the walls, the Fatimids tried to set it alight with a special fuel that creates what is known as Greek fire. This could not be put out with water. Christians from Jerusalem had advised the crusaders to use vinegar to put out Greek fire. The crusaders had stored plenty of vinegar in their siege tower and were able to quench the flames.

Around midday, the crusaders made a remarkable breakthrough. Fire broke out further along the wall. When the Fatimids facing the siege tower rushed to put it out, Godfrey took his chance. He quickly cut a section from the siege tower and used it to make a bridge to the wall. The crusaders from the siege tower rushed over the bridge while others began to climb the walls using scaling ladders. The crusaders were in.

> ### Reflect
> The fourteenth-century illustration on page 88 shows the crusaders entering Jerusalem on 15 July 1099. What details has the artist included to portray the religious and military aspects of the conquest?

The sack of Jerusalem

When the crusaders entered Jerusalem, Fatimid resistance collapsed almost at once. The city's commander, Iftikar ad-Daulah, concerned for his own safety, made a deal with the crusaders. He agreed to hand over the city immediately if he, his family and a small number of people close to him were allowed to leave. The crusaders appear to have kept their word.

The rest of Jerusalem's population was not so fortunate, however. As thousands of crusaders poured into Jerusalem on 15 July they unleashed violence and slaughter on a terrible scale. The sack of Jerusalem is one of the most horrific events of the Middle Ages. Some Latin chroniclers who recorded the events were shocked by what happened:

> **From Raymond of Aguilers's *History of the Franks who captured Jerusalem*, c.1101**
> Some of the pagans were mercifully beheaded, others pierced by arrows plunged from towers, and yet others, tortured for a long time, were burned to death in searing flames. Piles of heads, hands and feet lay in the houses and streets, and men and knights were running to and fro over corpses.

> **From Fulcher of Chartres, *A History of the Expedition to Jerusalem, 1095–1127*, c.1106**
> If you had been there, your feet would have been stained to the ankles in the blood of the slain. What shall I say? None of them were left alive. Neither women nor children were spared.

Crusader violence paid no attention to sacred refuges in the city. Many Muslims and Jews were murdered in the mosques and synagogues. The crusaders turned to plunder as well as killing. One chronicler reported that Tancred of Hauteville rushed into the Temple of Solomon and grabbed all the gold, silver and precious jewels that he could carry. After the slaughter, laden with captured booty, crusaders did penance and worshipped in the Holy Sepulchre. The historian Thomas Asbridge has tried to get into the minds of the crusaders to explain this mixture of violence, greed and piety.

> **Thomas Asbridge, *The First Crusade: A New History*, 2004**
> A modern observer might be forgiven for imagining that no flame of Christian devotion could possibly continue to burn amid such a storm of greed and violence. Not so. For the sack of Jerusalem proves one thing beyond contestation – in the minds of the crusaders, religious fervour, barbaric warfare and a self-serving desire for material gain were not separate experiences, but could all exist, entwined, in the same time and space.

> ### Reflect
> How useful are the sources and interpretation on this page for studying the massacre at Jerusalem?

Record

As you read through this final section, make more explanation cards to show what helped and what hindered the crusaders as they tried to establish the Kingdom of Jerusalem.

Reflect

How does the interpretation in this image differ from the picture you have already seen on page 81?

▼ Godfrey being crowned as ruler of Jerusalem. A French trade card from the nineteenth century

● Establishing the Kingdom of Jerusalem

The crusaders were overjoyed at their capture of Jerusalem, but in the aftermath of their victory they were faced with some difficult questions:

- How could the territory around Jerusalem be secured?
- Who should lead the new kingdom?
- How could the crusaders establish permanent Christian rule in the Holy Land?

In the eighteenth months which followed the conquest of Jerusalem, the crusaders began to answer these questions.

Creating a kingdom

Following the crusaders' victory, the Byzantine Patriarch of Jerusalem fled to Cyprus. The selection of his successor was a chance to heal or worsen relations with the Byzantines. The choice of a Norman patriarch marked an open attack on the principle of Byzantine control of the Church in the Holy Land. The new patriarch expelled eastern Christians from the Church of the Holy Sepulchre and soon began to persecute them throughout the Holy Land. To Alexios, this was an open attack.

Two great leaders of the crusade stood in contention for being the secular ruler of Jerusalem: Raymond of Toulouse and Godfrey of Bouillon. Raymond wanted to become the King of Jerusalem, but he had lost the support of many crusaders and it was Godfrey who was chosen. Raymond's piety had led him to believe that there could only ever be one King of Jerusalem: Jesus Christ. Godfrey skilfully rejected the title of 'King'. Instead, on 23 July 1099, he became 'Advocate of the Holy Sepulchre'. It was now down to him to establish the Kingdom of Jerusalem.

How did the crusaders establish the Kingdom of Jerusalem?

Supply lines

The conquest of Jerusalem had a dramatic impact on the population of Palestine. Many Muslims fled from towns and cities across the region. This had a negative impact on food production and trade. Although some crucial supplies had arrived through the nearest port of Jaffa in June 1099, the supply lines to the crusaders were precarious. Godfrey knew that it was essential to keep Jerusalem supplied with food and other provisions if the crusaders were to establish themselves permanently in the Holy Land.

In their final rush to reach Jerusalem, the crusaders had failed to secure the ports along the coast of the Mediterranean, but these would be crucial supply lines in the new crusader state. Merchants from Genoa and Venice had already played an important role in supplying the First Crusade. Now they were pleased to further increase their profits by keeping the new crusader colony supplied. But support from the Genoese and Venetian merchants came at a price. These men demanded extensive property in the ports which supplied the new kingdom.

Support from Europe

In the late summer of 1099, most crusaders felt that their work had been done. They had survived the 2000-mile pilgrimage to Jerusalem and had succeeded in establishing Christian control over the city. Of the tens of thousands of people who had left Europe three years earlier, perhaps only one-tenth had survived. Most of these now returned home. This left a few hundred knights and foot soldiers, who remained very vulnerable.

The crusaders who returned to Europe were often poor and exhausted, but they carried with them palm fronds from Jerusalem and wonderful stories of suffering and valour. When Godfrey of Bouillon sent appeals to Latin Christendom for reinforcements in the autumn of 1099, it is not surprising that his pleas for help fell on fertile ground. A huge number of armed men were keen to show their support for the new crusader colony, but it would be several months before they arrived in the Holy Land.

> **Reflect**
>
> What helped and what hindered the crusaders as they tried to establish the Kingdom of Jerusalem?

▶ The crusader Kingdom of Jerusalem in the early twelfth century

The Muslim threat

In the Islamic world there was shock and horror at the fall of Jerusalem. This was the first time the city had been in Christian hands since AD638. Yet there was no unified Muslim response. For the Abbasid caliph in Baghdad the arrival of the crusaders in distant Jerusalem was not a serious concern. The priority for the Seljuk sultan in Iran was extending his territory. Neither of these Muslim leaders sent armies to protect Jerusalem. The lack of unity in the Islamic world was extremely helpful to the crusaders as they tried to establish the Kingdom of Jerusalem. However, they continued to face a major threat from the Fatimids.

Ascalon

Fatimid forces led by Al Afdal arrived from Egypt at the port of Ascalon (see map on page 91) in early August 1099. They were too late to save the population of Jerusalem, but were determined to claim back their territory. This Fatimid military threat was a serious challenge to the security of Jerusalem and the new crusader state. The Fatimids had an army of over 10,000. It was a powerful multi-ethnic force with huge numbers of cavalry.

By the time the Fatimids arrived at Ascalon, Raymond of Toulouse and Godfrey of Bouillon were once again in dispute. Some of the crusader leaders had left, meaning that Godfrey had only 300 knights to defend Jerusalem. Those who remained continued to argue. When Tancred of Hauteville captured a group of Fatimid scouts he discovered that Al Afdal was at Ascalon, but not all of the remaining crusader leaders were convinced of the need to act. Godfrey and Robert of Flanders marched alone out of Jerusalem to face their opponents. Only after Godfrey's urgent appeals, and under pressure from their followers, did Raymond of Toulouse and Robert of Normandy decide to set out for Ascalon on 10 August.

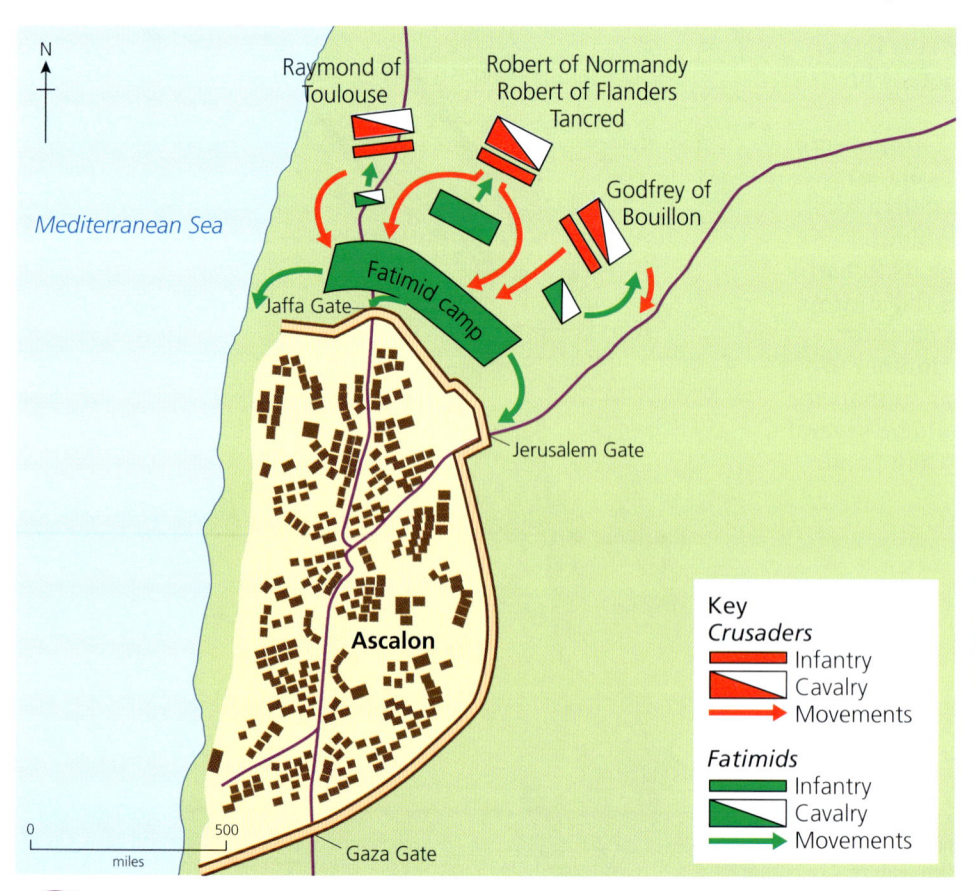

Al Afdal's troops, including his powerful cavalry, had already set up a defensive camp outside the fortified city walls. Although the crusader force was significantly smaller in number, its men had been victorious with far worse odds. What was certain was that there was no second chance: victory or death were their only outcomes.

◀ The Battle of Ascalon

> ### Reflect
> What hindered the crusaders as they faced the threat from the Fatimids?

How did the crusaders establish the Kingdom of Jerusalem?

The Battle of Ascalon

Godfrey knew that the outnumbered crusader force had to rely on an element of surprise if it were to stand any chance of success. At dawn on 12 August he launched a sudden attack on the still-sleeping Fatimid troops camping outside Jaffa Gate. This gave the Fatimids no time to organise their cavalry. Robert of Normandy charged at the camp and captured Al Afdal's personal standard. While the crusaders argued over the spoils of the camp, Al Afdal managed to rally some troops for a counter-attack, but Godfrey of Bouillon's men drove them off.

It was a savage battle. Some of the Fatimids fled to the port, only to be massacred by Raymond's men. Some hid at the top of palm trees, only to be shot out of them by crusader archers. Some tried to take refuge within the city walls, only to be crushed by the crowd all forcing themselves through the city gates. Al Afdal and a few of his officers managed to escape back to Egypt, leaving behind what remained of the Muslim garrison.

Abandoned by their leaders, the remaining Fatimid fighters were more than willing to surrender. They insisted on negotiating with Raymond of Toulouse as he was known to have kept his promises during the sack of Jerusalem. Godfrey was afraid that Raymond would use this opportunity to establish his own territory around Ascalon and therefore interfered in the negotiations. As a result, Ascalon remained in Muslim hands.

Despite this the crusaders returned to Jerusalem in triumph. In the Church of the Holy Sepulchre they praised God for their victory and raised Al Afdal's captured green standard in the church as a permanent reminder of their success.

> ### Reflect
> How does this 1839 painting by a French artist portray the scene of Godfrey of Bouillon depositing the trophies of Ascalon in the Church of the Holy Sepulchre as an important event?

▼ Godfrey of Bouillon depositing the trophies of Ascalon in the Holy Sepulchre Church, Jerusalem, August 1099, by the French artist Francois-Marius Granet, 1839

Divisions, dangers and deaths

Despite their victory at Ascalon, divisions within the crusader leadership meant that they did not take full advantage of their success. Ascalon should have provided a much needed, secure port for trade and supplies. Instead, Raymond and Godfrey's quarrels about who should control the city allowed the Muslim garrison of Ascalon to hold its position. Ascalon remained under Muslim control, and added to the vulnerability of the emerging crusader state.

In the autumn of 1099, Godfrey of Bouillon's future looked bleak. Few of his knights remained and Fatimid power was far from broken. He knew that it was important to establish a secure port to supply Jerusalem, but a long siege of the port of Arsuf failed. When he returned to Jerusalem in early December, his position as ruler of Jerusalem came under threat.

Just before Christmas, three ambitious men arrived in Jerusalem to visit the holy sites:

- Bohemond of Taranto travelled from Antioch.
- Godfrey's brother, Baldwin of Boulogne, made the long journey from Edessa.
- The new papal representative, Daimbert of Pisa, also arrived in Jerusalem.

Each of these men had hopes of ruling the new kingdom. Godfrey only managed to hold onto power by making Daimbert the new Patriarch of Jerusalem. Once again, divisions among the leaders had hindered the success of the First Crusade.

The following summer, Godfrey fell ill after eating oranges at the palace of the Muslim ruler of Caesarea. Some people suspected poisoning, but it is more likely that he had caught typhoid. On 18 July, Godfrey confessed his sins and died five days later. His body was buried in the entrance to the Church of the Holy Sepulchre.

Baldwin I

Godfrey of Bouillon's death created turmoil in the emerging Kingdom of Jerusalem as people wondered who might seize power. It was Godfrey's wish that the kingdom should pass to his younger brother, Baldwin of Boulogne. In September 1100, messengers arrived in Edessa to invite Baldwin to be the new ruler of the Kingdom of Jerusalem. Baldwin was delighted at this opportunity to extend his power. In October he left Edessa and marched south to Jerusalem with just 200 knights and 700 infantrymen. Unlike his brother, Baldwin had no reservations about taking the title of 'King'. He was crowned in the Church of the Nativity on Christmas Day 1100.

Reflect

What helped and what hindered Godfrey of Bouillon as the first ruler of Jerusalem?

Record

Finish your explanation cards to show what helped and what hindered the crusaders as they tried to establish the Kingdom of Jerusalem.

How did the crusaders establish the Kingdom of Jerusalem?

◀ The funeral of Godfrey of Bouillon and coronation of Baldwin I, from a thirteenth-century edition of William of Tyre's *History of the Kingdom of Jerusalem*, c.1184

After 1100

In the 200 years after Baldwin's coronation, the Latin Christians extended their territory in Palestine and Syria. But controlling the crusader states was never easy. In the twelfth century the Islamic world came together and placed the crusader states under increasing pressure. Between 1100 and 1292 at least eight more crusades left Europe to defend the Holy Land. In the end they failed. By the end of 1292, the Muslim victory was complete and the crusaders' rule in Palestine and Syria had ended.

Review

1. Arrange your explanation cards under different headings. You may find the following helpful:
   - Divisions in the Islamic world
   - The religious devotion of the crusaders
   - The military tactics of the crusaders
   - Help from outsiders
   - Divisions between the leaders of the crusade
   - The military power of the Fatimids
   - Conditions in Syria and Palestine.
2. Which of the factors do you think was most important in helping the crusaders to succeed?
3. **'Divisions between the leaders almost wrecked the First Crusade.'** How far do you agree with this statement? Write an essay to explain your answer.

CLOSER LOOK 5

Islamic perspectives on the First Crusade

Most studies of the First Crusade rely heavily on European sources for details of the events. In comparison, Islamic perspectives on the First Crusade are less widely used. Two reasons for this are:

1. There are relatively few Muslim accounts of the First Crusade. No texts survive from the time of the First Crusade itself. Later chronicles from the twelfth and thirteenth centuries tend to be general studies of history which contain only brief mentions of the First Crusade.
2. Most historians who research and write about the First Crusade are from the west. Often they cannot read Arabic and do not have detailed knowledge of the Islamic texts.

In recent years, some western historians *have* attempted to use Muslim texts that refer to the First Crusade. The following two case studies of Islamic perspectives show that these can provide interesting insights into different aspects of the First Crusade.

Case study 1: The causes of the First Crusade

This is the magnificent Great Mosque in Damascus which was constructed by the Umayyads in the early eighth century. In the years just after the First Crusade, a scholar called Al-Sulami taught here. Around 1105, Al-Sulami gave a number of lectures about the threat that Islam faced from western Christians. He recorded these views in his *Book of Holy War*.

▶ The Great Mosque in Damascus

Reflect
According to Al-Sulami, what made the crusaders invade Syria?

From Al-Sulami's *Book of Holy War*, c.1105
A number of the enemy pounced on the island of Sicily while the Muslims disputed and competed, and they conquered in the same way one city after another in al-Andalus. When reports confirmed for them that Syria suffered from the disagreement of its master and rulers, they set out for it, and Jerusalem was their dearest wish.

Case study 2: The conquest of Jerusalem

No Muslim texts about the conquest of Jerusalem were written at the time. However, during the twelfth and thirteenth centuries, several chroniclers described the events of July 1099. Over time, their accounts of the devastation caused by the crusaders became more and more extreme, as you can see in the examples below:

Ibn al-Qalanisi writing c.1190
The Franks stormed the town and gained possession of it. A number of the townsfolk fled to the sanctuary and were killed.

Ibn al-Jawzi writing in 1200
Among the events in this year was the taking of Jerusalem by the Franks on Friday 13 Sha/'ban (15 July). They killed more than 70,000 Muslims there. They took forty-odd silver candelabra from the Dome of the Rock, each one worth 360,000 dirhams. They took a silver lamp weighing forty Syrian ratls. They took twenty-odd gold lamps, innumerable items of clothing and other things.

Ibn al-Athir writing in 1233
The Franks killed more than 70,000 people in the Aqsa mosque, among them a large group of Muslim imams, religious scholars and devout men from amongst those who had left their homelands and lived in the vicinity of the Holy Place.

> **Reflect**
>
> What can we learn from these extracts about what happened at the Dome of the Rock and the Aqsa Mosque?
>
> Why do you think historians have to be careful when using such accounts?

◀ The Aqsa Mosque, Jerusalem

The study of Islamic perspectives is one way in which we can gain a richer understanding of the First Crusade. Historical research does not stand still. New generations of historians build on the work of earlier scholars by working on new sources, asking new questions and developing new ideas. Their work helps us to understand the experiences and attitudes of people on different sides of the conflict.

Preparing for the examination

The world depth study forms the second half of Paper 3: World History. It is worth 20 per cent of your GCSE. To succeed in the examination, you will need to think clearly about different aspects of The First Crusade, c.1070–1100 and support your ideas with accurate knowledge. This section suggests some revision strategies you might like to try and explains the types of examination questions that you can expect.

● Summaries of the five key issues

Your study of The First Crusade, c.1070–1100, has covered five important issues:

1. Origins
2. Responses, November 1095 to December 1096
3. Into Asia Minor, December 1096 to October 1097
4. Antioch, October 1097 to June 1098
5. Jerusalem, July 1098 to July 1100

In the specification for your GCSE course, each of the five issues is divided into three sections. We divided each enquiry in this book into three stages to match these sections and to help you build your knowledge and understanding step by step.

Now you can use your knowledge and understanding to produce a detailed and accurate summary for each of the five issues. You will also need to be clear about how the five issues are connected. Here are four suggestions for structuring your revision notes and showing the connections between the issues. Choose the one that is best for you, or use a variety if you prefer.

1. Mind maps

A mind map on A3 paper (or even larger) is a good way to summarise the important points about a particular issue. It allows you to show connections between different points. Make five mind maps, one for each enquiry. Your first might look something like this:

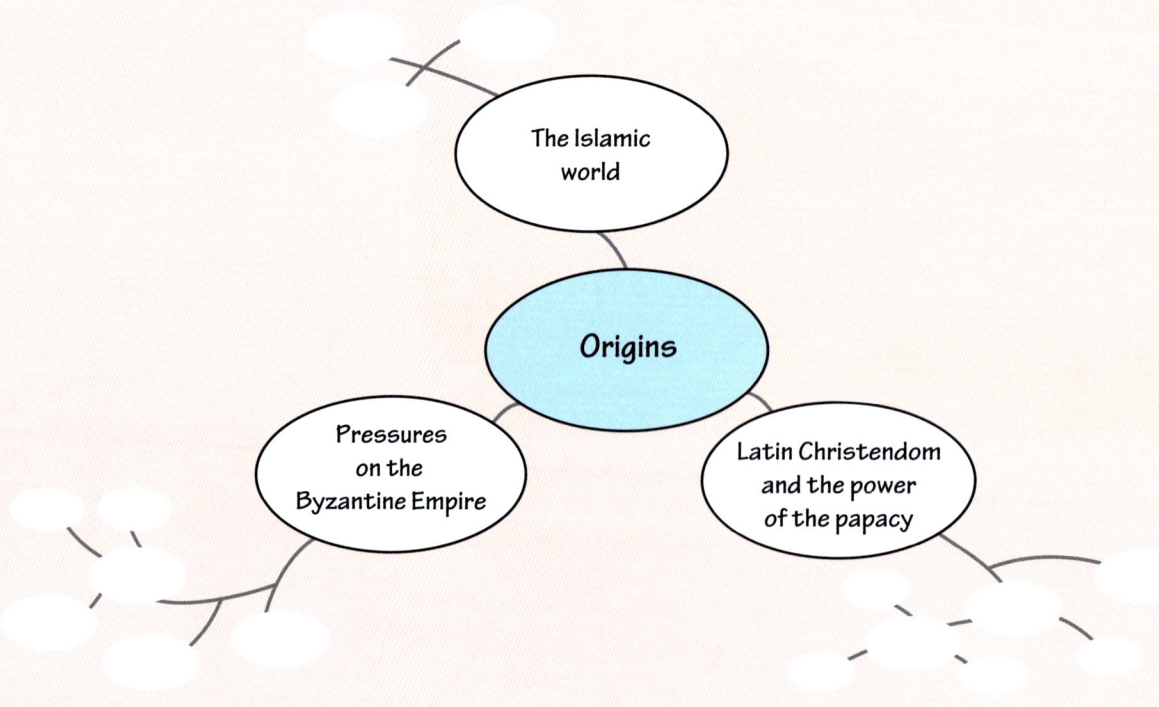

```
         The Islamic
            world
              |
           Origins
          /       \
  Pressures       Latin Christendom
   on the         and the power
Byzantine Empire  of the papacy
```

2. Charts

If you find it easier to learn from lists then a summary chart for each issue you have studied might be best for you. You can use the format shown below or design your own. Just make sure that you include clear summary points for each of the three sections in each enquiry you studied.

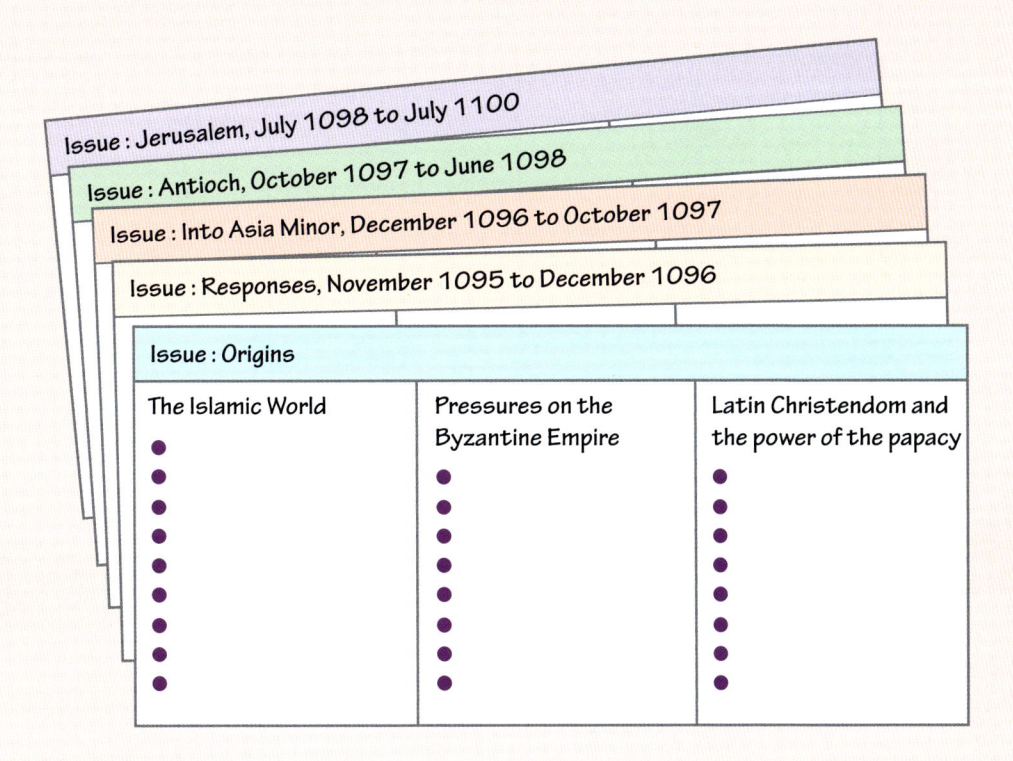

Issue: Jerusalem, July 1098 to July 1100

Issue: Antioch, October 1097 to June 1098

Issue: Into Asia Minor, December 1096 to October 1097

Issue: Responses, November 1095 to December 1096

Issue: Origins

The Islamic World	Pressures on the Byzantine Empire	Latin Christendom and the power of the papacy
• • • • • •	• • • • • •	• • • • • •

3. Small cards

Small cards are a flexible way to make revision notes. You could create a set of revision cards for each of the five main issues/enquiries you have studied. It would be a good idea to use a different colour for each set of cards.

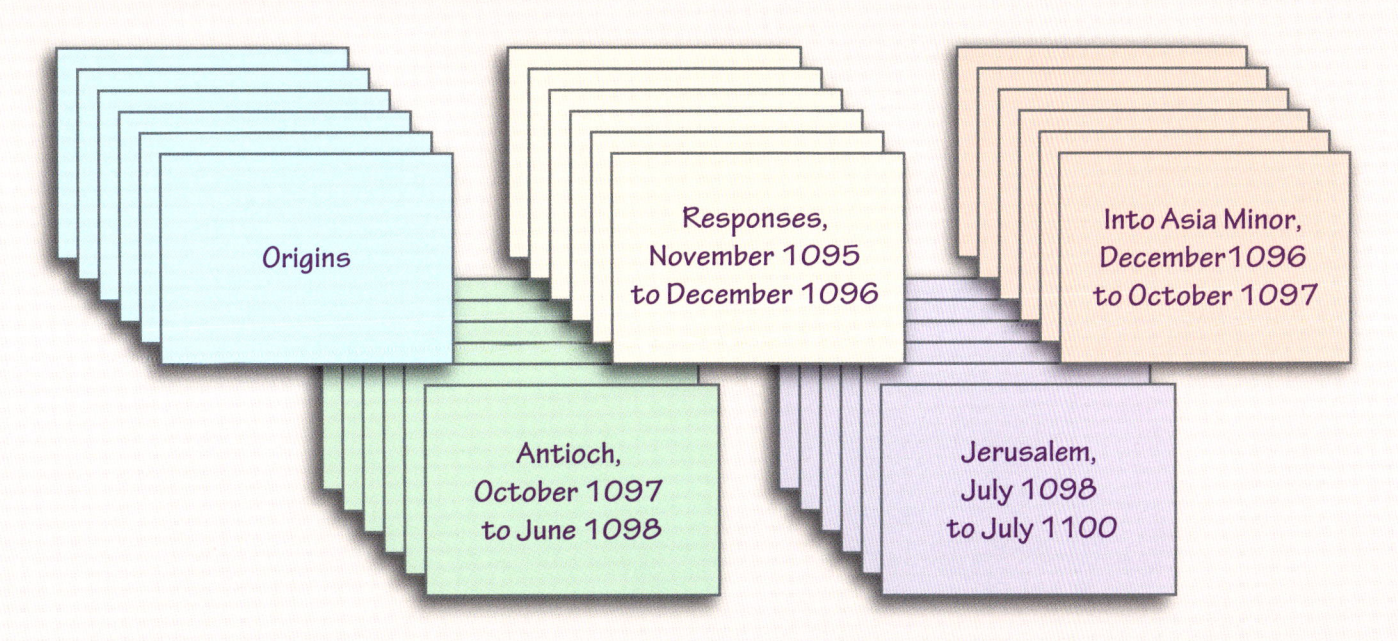

- Origins
- Responses, November 1095 to December 1096
- Into Asia Minor, December 1096 to October 1097
- Antioch, October 1097 to June 1098
- Jerusalem, July 1098 to July 1100

4. Podcasts

If you learn best by listening to information and explanations, you could record your knowledge and understanding by producing podcasts to summarise what you have learned about each of the five main issues. You could produce your podcast with a friend using a question-and-answer format.

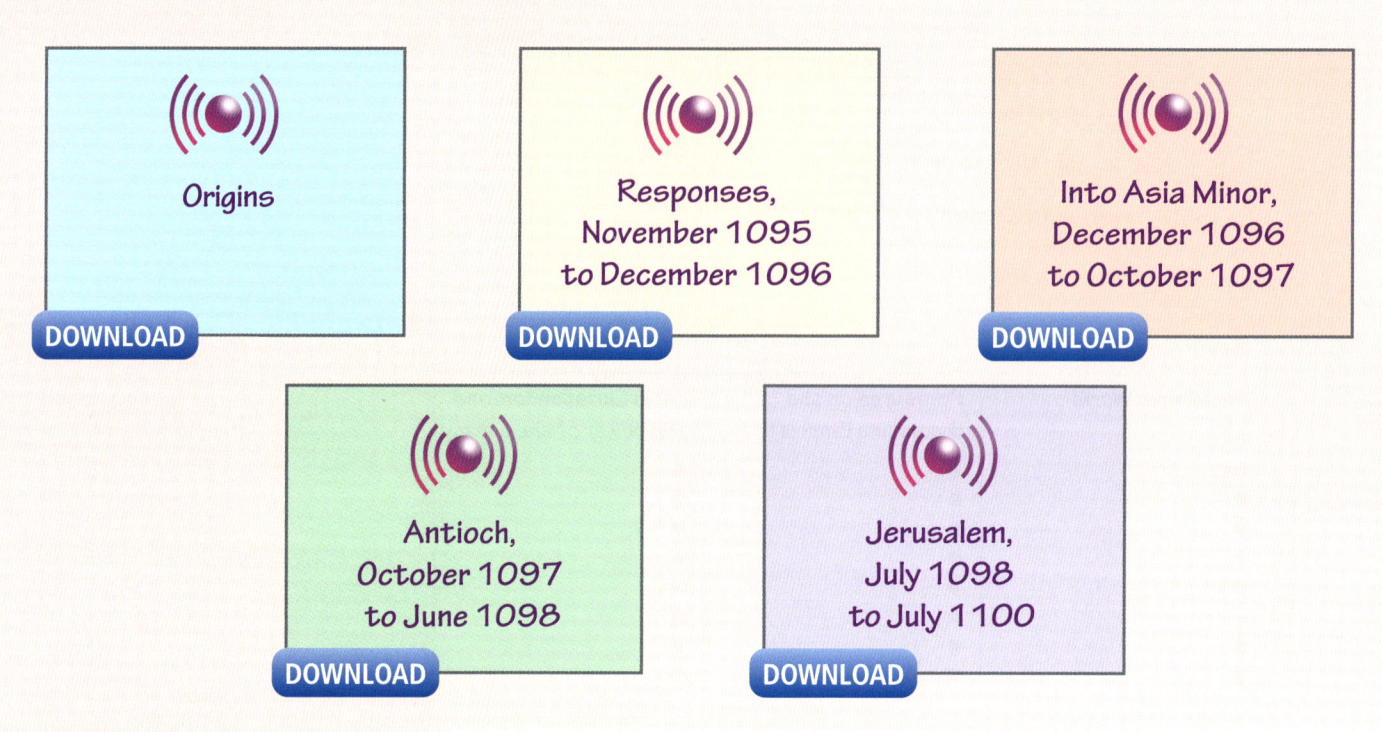

- Origins — DOWNLOAD
- Responses, November 1095 to December 1096 — DOWNLOAD
- Into Asia Minor, December 1096 to October 1097 — DOWNLOAD
- Antioch, October 1097 to June 1098 — DOWNLOAD
- Jerusalem, July 1098 to July 1100 — DOWNLOAD

To be well-prepared for the examination you need revision notes that summarise the main points and provide detailed examples in a format that works best for you.

Preparing for the examination

● Exam guidance

This depth study forms the second half of Paper 3: World History. It is worth 20 per cent of your GCSE. The whole exam lasts for 1 hour and 45 minutes so you will have just over 50 minutes to answer the three questions on The First Crusade, c.1070–1100.

Question 6

You will be given a single source to analyse. This will focus on an aspect of the First Crusade that you have studied. The source could be an extract from a written document or an image. The question will always be 'What can Source A tell us about…?'. To answer the question you will need to refer to the details in the source and use your own knowledge.

Example

6. What can Source A tell us about the Battle of Dorylaeum? Use the source and your own knowledge to support your answer. (7)

> **SOURCE A From *The Deeds of the Franks*, first published c.1100. An account of the Battle of Dorylaeum. It was written by a Christian soldier who was there at the time. The battle took place in July 1097 as the crusaders were crossing Muslim lands in what is now Turkey.**
>
> The Turks came at us from all sides, brandishing their weapons and hurling them and shooting arrows from an incredible distance. We knew we could not withstand them or hold the weight of so many enemies, but we went forward to meet them as one. Our women were a great help to us that day, bringing water to drink for the fighters and encouraging those who were fighting and defending … Our men asked in astonishment where such a multitude of Turks, Arabs, Saracens and others whose name I do not know had come from, because all the mountains, hills and valleys were filled with these people. Then a secret message was sent out among us … stating, 'Come what may, stand firm in the faith of Christ and have faith in the victory of the Holy Cross, because today, if it pleases God, all riches shall be given you.'

Practise this type of question using the example above.

1. What exactly does this source reveal about:
   ● how the Turks fought
   ● how the crusaders fought
   ● the nature and number of the Turkish army
   ● what gave the crusaders strength?
2. What are the limitations of the source in terms of what it can tell us about the battle?
3. Make sure you use some of your own knowledge about the Battle of Dorylaeum to analyse the source.

Question 7

You will be given a collection of sources and interpretations to analyse. These could be two sources and an interpretation or two interpretations and a source. The collection will focus on an aspect of the First Crusade that you have studied. It may include visual as well as written sources and interpretations. The question stem will always be 'How useful are Interpretation B and Sources C and D (or Source B and Interpretations C and D) for a historian studying...?' To answer the question you will need to refer to the details in the interpretation/sources and use your own knowledge.

Example

7. How useful are Source B and Interpretations C and D for a historian studying how the crusaders survived the siege of Antioch in June 1098? In your answer, refer to the source and the two interpretations as well as your own knowledge. (15)

SOURCE B From the chronicle of Raymond of Aguilers, written c.1101. A crusader's account of how they discovered an ancient object under the floor of a church in Antioch where they were under siege. Many of them believed that they had found the Holy Lance that pierced Christ's side as he died on the cross.

After we had dug from morning to evening, some began to despair of finding the Lance. The youth who had spoken of the Lance, saw that we were worn out, and took off his shoes and coat and descended into the pit in his shirt, earnestly begging us to pray that God would give us his Lance for the comfort and victory of His people. Finally, in His mercy, the Lord showed us His Lance. And I, who have written this, kissed it when the point alone had as yet appeared above ground. What great joy and exultation then filled the city I cannot describe … When our men felt defeated, discouraged and under severe pressure, this divine aid appeared.

INTERPRETATION C From *The Crusades* by Thomas Asbridge, 2010. Historian Thomas Asbridge writes about the Battle of Antioch that ended the siege on 28 June 1098.

The Battle of Antioch was a stunning victory. Never before had the crusade come so close to destruction and yet, against all expectation, Christendom had triumphed. Not surprisingly, many saw the hand of God at work and an array of spectacular miracles was reported. It was said that an army of ghostly Christian martyrs, clad all in white and led by soldier saints appeared out of the mountains to aid the Franks. Elsewhere on the battlefield, Raymond of Aguilers himself carried the Holy Lance in among the southern French contingent led by Bishop Adhemar. It was later said that the sight of the relic paralysed Kerbogha, the Muslim leader.

Preparing for the examination

INTERPRETATION D From a version of the chronicle of William of Tyre, made between 1232 and 1261. The illustration shows the battle at Antioch (June 1098). Bishop Adhemar, a crusader leader, is shown on the left, carrying the Holy Lance.

Practise this type of question by using the example above.

1. Make sure you think about the interpretations and source in relation to the focus of study identified in the question: how the crusaders survived the siege of Antioch in June 1098.
2. Study the interpretations and source carefully and decided what aspects of the crusaders' survival during the siege they help us to understand.
3. What exactly do the interpretations and source tell us about: a) the crusaders' reaction to the discovery of the Holy Lance; b) who carried the lance into the battle; c) the reasons that the crusaders gave for their survival and victory at Antioch?
4. Analyse the interpretations and source, and use your own knowledge, to think about any limitations in what they can tell us about the crusaders' survival during the siege.
5. Make an overall judgement about how useful the interpretations and source are for a historian studying the crusaders' survival during the siege.

Question 8/9

You have a choice of two judgement questions: Question 8 or Question 9. These questions in the second part of Paper 3 are the most challenging because they ask you to make a judgement about an aspect of the First Crusade, 1070–1100. The question will always ask how far you agree with a given statement. You need to save enough time for this question because it is worth 18 marks.

Examples

8. 'The People's Crusade of 1095–1096 was a catastrophic failure.' How far do you agree with this view? (18)

9. 'The Islamic world was hopelessly weak and divided in the years just before the First Crusade'. How far do you agree with this view? (18)

You may wish to agree completely or disagree completely or take a position where you can see some reasons for agreeing and some for disagreeing. You can get full marks for any of these types of answer provided that you:

- show that you have fully understood the given statement
- use very clear explanations and suitable accurate supporting evidence to persuade the examiner that you are giving a very reasonable answer
- keep closely to the point all the way through your answer.

Choose one of the example questions above and write a plan of how you would answer it. It is helpful to plan each paragraph in your answer so that it has a very definite main point that is clearly supported with accurate and appropriate evidence chosen from your knowledge of the period.

Preparing for the examination

● Sources and interpretations

A **source** is a written document, picture, artefact or site which was created by people at the time. Sources such as chronicles, letters, charters and artefacts provide a wealth of evidence about the First Crusade, c.1070–1100.

An **interpretation** is any version of events in the past that has been created at some later time. Interpretations such as books and articles written by historians, documentaries, websites, exhibitions, monuments, novels and films provide a range of different perspectives on the First Crusade, c.1070–1100.

In this book you have studied a wide range of historical sources and interpretations relating to different aspects of the First Crusade.

1. Select a source from each of the enquiries you have studied. It would be good to choose a mixture of written and visual sources. For each source devise a question 6: 'What can Source A tell us about…?'.
2. On page 47 you will find a nineteenth-century oil painting of Godfrey swearing his oath to Alexios as well as an extract from a letter by Stephen of Blois. This interpretation and source both concern Alexios I and his relationship with the crusade leaders. Do an online search for an additional source about this same issue (for example, from a chronicle about the crusade written before or soon after 1100) and then devise a question 7: How useful are Interpretation B and Sources C and D for a historian studying…?'.

Copyright information:

Source A: Adapted from Nirmal Dass, *The Deeds of the Franks and Other Jerusalem-Bound Pilgrims: The Earliest Chronicle of the First Crusade*, pg 42, Rowman & Littlefield Publishers, USA, 2011.

Source B: Adapted from August C Krey, *The First Crusade, the Accounts of Eye-Witnesses and Participants*, pg 181, Princeton University Press, USA, 1921.

Interpretation C: Adapted from Thomas Asbridge, *The Crusades: The War for the Holy Land*, pg 81, Simon & Schuster Inc, London, 2010.

Interpretation D: Detail of a miniature of the battle outside Antioch. Origin: France, N. (Picardy?). Image freely available from The British Library Images Online, www.imagesonline.bl.uk

Glossary

Abbasids the Muslim family that ruled as caliphs of Islam between 750 and 1258

al-Andaulus the area of modern Spain which was under Muslim rule from c.750

alms money given to help the poor

Anatolia the central part of Asia Minor

anti-Semitism hostility or prejudice towards Jews

Asia Minor the area of land that occupies most of modern Turkey, sometimes referred to as Anatolia

Balkans the region in south-east Europe between Greece and the Black Sea

ballista siege weapon like a huge crossbow, used to hurl large stones at the enemy

barbarians group of people considered to be uncivilised or primitive

battering ram a siege engine used for breaking down stone walls or wooden gates

Byzantine Empire the eastern half of the Roman Empire that survived after the collapse of the Roman Empire in the west

caliph the title of the ruler of Islam after the death of the Prophet Muhammad

cavalry soldiers who fight on horseback

chalice the wine cup used in the Christian mass. The original chalice was used by Christ at the last supper

charter a document giving someone certain rights, e.g. over property or trade

chronicle a written account

chronicler the writer of a chronicle

cistern storage tank for water

citadel a fortress

Dome of the Rock the Muslim shrine built on the site in Jerusalem from where Muslims believed Muhammad began his Night Journey

excommunicate expel from full membership of the Roman Catholic Church

Fatimids the Muslim rulers of Tunisia and Egypt between 909 and 1191

forage search for food

Franks the name given to crusaders by Muslims

garrison a group of soldiers who protect a town or fortress

Greek fire clay pots filled with flammable sulphur and oils

heathen a person who does not believe in the Christian God

hippodrome an area used for chariot-racing

Holy Lance the lance that Christians believe was used to pierce the side of Jesus as he hung on the cross

Holy Land the name given by Christians to the area around Jerusalem and Bethlehem where Jesus lived and died

Holy Sepulchre the church in Jerusalem built close to the site where Jesus was crucified and buried

Holy War a war that is fought to defend a particular religion

Islam the name of the Muslim religion

knight a minor nobleman

Latin Christendom the part of Europe under the spiritual leadership of the pope

mangonel a tall wooden catapult used for hurling large stones

massacre the deliberate and brutal slaughter of many people

mercenaries hired soldiers who are prepared to fight for any cause in return for payment

military coup when soldiers remove a ruler from power and take control

monastery a community of monks living under religious vows

monk a man who serves God by living and praying with other monks in a monastery

Night Journey the name Muslims give to Muhammad's journey to heaven and back from Jerusalem

noble a powerful lord

pagans people who worship spirits rather than a single God

papacy the office of the pope

Patriarch a leader of the Christian Church, most often used in the Byzantine Church

peasant poor farm worker

penance confessing sin and being granted forgiveness in return for doing acts that show a genuine desire to cleanse the soul

penitence acts such as fasting or going on pilgrimage to gain forgiveness for sins

piety religious devotion

pilgrim person who goes on a pilgrimage

pilgrimage a journey to a holy place

pitch tar

pogrom an attack on Jews

Pope the leader of the Latin Church

purgatory a place where, according to Christian belief, the souls of the dead are cleansed by suffering before they can enter heaven

relic an item or body part associated with a dead saint

sappers soldiers who dig tunnels beneath walls and towers

Seljuk Turks a tribe from central Asia who moved eastwards into Asia Minor during the eleventh century

Shi'ites one of the two main groups of Muslims (the other being Sunni). Shi'ites insist that the leadership of the Muslim world must pass down the family line of the Prophet Muhammad

shrine a spiritual place with a connection to a holy person or relic

siege engines large weapons used to attack a town or fortress

siege tower a wooden tower which protected soldiers as they attacked the walls of a town or fortress

sin breaking the rules of the Church

Sultan the highest rank of Muslim below the caliph

Sunni one of the two main groups of Muslims (the other being Shi'ite). Sunni Muslims believe that the leadership of the Muslim world should be held by those most suited to the role and that leaders do not need to be descended from the Prophet Muhammad

warlord a military leader who controlled a large territory

Index

Abbasids 11, 13, 92
Adhemar, Bishop of Le Puy 25, 29, 34, 44, 73, 80
    and Antioch 66, 71, 72, 76, 77
Al Afdal 92, 93
al-Andalus 15, 23
Albert of Aachen 38
Alexios I Komnenos 18–19, 23, 27, 44, 57
    and Antioch 69, 82
    assistance to crusaders 48–9
    and Crusade leaders 46–9
    and Nicaea 53
    and People's Crusade 40–1
Al-Sulami: *Book of Holy War* 96
Anatolia 11, 17, 19, 56
Anna Komnena: *The Alexiad* 18, 25, 46, 48, 70
Antioch 19, 57, 62–77
    capture of 68–71
    massacre at 71
    siege of 64–7
Antioch, Battle of 76–7
anti-Semitism 39, 40
Aqsa Mosque, Jerusalem 12, 97
Armenians 58–9
Ascalon, Battle of 92–3
Asia Minor: journey across 56–9

Baghdad 13, 14
Baldwin of Boulogne (later Count of Edessa) 25, 34, 57, 59
    and Antioch 67
    and Jerusalem 94, 95
Balkans 18
Bayeux Tapestry 20
Bertrand of Moncontour 36
Bohemond of Taranto 25, 34, 47, 54, 55, 57
    and Antioch 65, 66, 67, 68, 69, 70, 71, 72, 76, 80, 82
    and Jerusalem 94
    and leadership rivalry 80, 82, 83, 84
Buondelmonti, Cristoforo 16
Byzantine Empire 11, 16–19
Byzantine Church 17, 23
    and Seljuk Turks 14

charters 36
chronicles 24–5, 28, 37, 38, 43, 72, 73
Church of the Holy Sepulchre 8, 13, 21, 93, 94
Cibot, Edouard 94
Cilician expedition 57–8
Clement III, Pope 22
Conques abbey church 21
Constantine, Roman Emperor 16
Constantinople (Istanbul) 16, 40, 44, 46
Council of Clermont 36

Daimbert of Pisa 94
Dome of the Rock 8, 12, 97

Doré, Gustav 41, 61
Dorylaeum, Battle of 54–5

Edessa 59, 69
Ekkehard, German monk 37
Emich of Leiningen 38, 39, 40
ergotism 37

Fatimids 11, 13, 14, 85, 86–9, 92–3
feudal system 33
Fulcher of Chartres 25, 27, 28, 55, 56, 89

Gesta Francorum (anon) 25, 27, 49, 52, 56, 58, 66, 67, 69, 71, 74, 84
Godfrey of Bouillon 6, 34, 47, 52, 54, 56, 57
    and Antioch 67, 71
    and Arqa 85
    and Battle of Ascalon 92, 93
    death of 94
    and Jerusalem 80–1, 87, 88, 90, 91, 94
    and leadership rivalry 83, 92, 94
Gottschalk 40
Granet, François-Marius 93
Great Mosque, Damascus 96
Gregory VII, Pope 22, 23, 30
Guibert of Nogent 35, 38

Hagia Sophia, Constantinople 16, 18
Hakim, Fatimid Caliph 13
Henry I, King of England 43
Henry IV, Holy Roman Emperor 22, 34
Hesse, Alexandre 47
Holy Lance 72–6, 77, 83, 85
holy war 22, 30
Hugh of Vermandois 46, 54

Ibn al-Athir 15, 75, 97
Ibn al-Jawzi 97
Ibn al-Qalanisi 97
Iftikar ad-Daulah 86, 89
Islam 8
    divisions in 13
    and Jerusalem 12
    perspectives on First Crusade 96–7
Islamic world 11, 12–15

Jerusalem 8–9, 80–1
    capture of 6–7, 86–9, 97
    and Islam 12
    journey from Antioch 84–5
    sack of 89
Jerusalem, Kingdom of: establishment of 90–5
Jews: attacks against 39, 40

Kerbogha, ruler of Mosul   69, 72–3, 76, 77
Kibotos   41, 48
Kilij Arslan, Sultan   50, 54, 55, 56
kings   33
knights   33, 35–6, 37
Knights of St Peter   22

Lariviere, Charles-Philippe   93
Latin Christendom   10, 16, 20–3
    Church Reform Movement   22, 34
    conflict with Byzantine Church   17, 23
    responses to crusade sermon   32–7

Madrazo, Federico de   81
Mainz massacre   39
Malik Shah   19
Manzikert, Battle of   14
Marrat an-Numan   84–5
Matthew of Edessa   75
monasticism   21

Neuville, Alphonse de   82
Nicaea   19, 50–3
Normans   15, 17, 18, 22

Omar of Azaz   83

Palestine   15
papacy   10, 20, 22–3
peasants   33, 37
penance   30, 32, 36, 49
penitence, acts of   21, 23, 30
People's Crusade   38–41
Peshnegs   17, 18
Peter Bartholomew   72–3, 85
Peter the Hermit   38, 39, 40, 44, 66, 76
pilgrimages   10, 21, 30, 31
pogroms   39, 40
princes   33, 34, 37, 46

Ralph of Caen   34, 75
Raymond of Aguilers   25, 50, 73, 74, 82, 89
Raymond of Toulouse   25, 29, 34, 47, 54, 56, 73
    and Antioch   65, 66, 67, 68, 69, 71, 72, 80, 82
    and Arqa   85
    and Battle of Ascalon   92, 93
    and Holy Lance   73, 83, 85
    and Jerusalem   85, 86, 90
    and leadership rivalry   80, 82, 83, 84, 92, 94
    and Marrat an-Numan   84
relics   21, 72–6, 77, 83, 85
Rhineland massacres   39
Robert of Flanders   54
    and Antioch   65, 66, 67, 71
    and Arqa   85

    and Battle of Ascalon   92
    and Jerusalem   87
Robert of Normandy (Robert Curthose)   25, 42–3, 54, 55, 92, 93

Seljuk Turks   8, 10, 14, 17, 19
    and Byzantine Empire   11, 14
    power struggle   65
Shi'ite Muslims   13
Sicily   15, 23
siege warfare   60–1
siege weapons   52, 87
Signol, Émile   7
Stephen of Blois   25, 47, 54, 63
    and Antioch   66, 72, 76
Stephen of Valence   72
Sunni Islam   13, 14
Syria   15

Tancred of Hauteville   34, 57, 92
    and Antioch   66, 67, 68, 71
    and Jerusalem   87, 89
Tatikios, Byzantine general   51, 54, 78–9
    siege of Antioch   66, 67, 68
Thoros, Count of Edessa   59
Toledo   15
Turkish warfare   54–5

Urban II, Pope   19, 23
    call to crusade   28–30
    and liberation of Jerusalem   31
    promise of forgiveness of sins   30
    sermon at Clermont   26–7, 28, 29
    tour of France   29

Volkmar   40

Walter Sans-Avoir   38, 39, 40
warfare
    siege warfare   60–1
    Turkish warfare   54–5
William of Tyre: *History of the Kingdom of Jerusalem*   6, 24, 77, 88
William Rufus, King of England   43
William the Carpenter   66

Yaghi Siyan   65, 66, 71

Acknowledgements

Text acknowledgements

p.36 Extract from Thomas Asbridge, *The Crusades* (Simon and Shuster, 2010); **p.52** Extract from Randall Rogers, *Latin Siege Warfare in the Twelfth Century* (Clarendon Press, 1997); **p.71** Extract from Christopher Tyerman, *God's War* (Penguin, 2007); **p.75** Extract from Thomas Asbridge, *The First Crusade: A New History* (Free Press, 2004); **p.78** Extracts from Thomas Asbridge, *The First Crusade: A New History* (Free Press, 2004) and Peter Frankopan, *The First Crusade: The Call from the East* (The Bodley Head, 2012); **p.89** Extract from Thomas Asbridge, *The First Crusade: A New History* (Free Press, 2004).

Picture credits

p.4 *t* © Ilan Shacham / Getty Images; *mtl* © Granger Historical Picture Archive / Alamy Stock Photo, *mbl* © Artur Bogacki / Alamy Stock Photo, *mr* Werner Forman / Universal Images Group / Getty Images; *bl* DeAgostini / Getty Images, *br* © Godong / Universal Images Group via Getty Images; **p.5** *tl* © DEA PICTURE LIBRARY / Getty Images, *tr* © Sonia Halliday Photo Library / Alamy Stock Photo, *m* Yates Thompson MS 12 Frontispiece to 'Histoire d'Outremer, continued to 1232' by William of Tyre, c.1232–61 (vellum), French School, (13th century) / British Library, London, UK / Bridgeman Images; **p.6** Yates Thompson MS 12 f.9v Initial 'a' depicting Godfrey de Bouillon and his train setting out on horseback, from 'William of Tyre, Histoire d'Outremer', 1232-61 (vellum), French School, (13th century) / British Library, London, UK / Bridgeman Images **p.7** © Christophel Fine Art / UIG via Getty Images; **pp.8–9** © Ilan Shacham / Getty Images; **p.12** © Zoonar GmbH / Alamy Stock Photo; **p.13** © DeAgostini / Getty Images; **p.14** © Westend61 GmbH / Alamy Stock Photo; **p.16** *t* © Granger Historical Picture Archive / Alamy Stock Photo, *b* © Artur Bogacki / Alamy Stock Photo; **p.17** © Werner Forman / Universal Images Group / Getty Images; **p.18** © INTERFOTO / Alamy Stock Photo; **p.19** © ART Collection / Alamy Stock Photo; **p.20** © DeAgostini / Getty Images; **p.21** © Godong / Universal Images Group via Getty Images; **p.22** © DEA PICTURE LIBRARY / Getty Images; **p.23** © Sonia Halliday Photo Library / Alamy Stock Photo; **p.24** Yates Thompson MS 12 Frontispiece to 'Histoire d'Outremer, continued to 1232' by William of Tyre, c.1232–61 (vellum), French School, (13th century) / British Library, London, UK / Bridgeman Images; **p.26** © Universal History Archive / UIG via Getty Images; **p.28** © Bernard Jaubert / Getty Images; **p.29** *b* © Keystone-France / Gamma-Keystone via Getty Images; **p.30** © INTERFOTO / Alamy Stock Photo; **p.31** © DeAgostini / Getty Images; **p.32** © DeAgostini / Getty Images; **p.33** *t* Public domain, *tm* © Leema via Getty Images, *bm* © GUIZIOU Franck / hemis.fr / Getty Images, *b* © Fine Art Images / Heritage Images / Getty Images; **p.35** © Fratelli Alinari; **p.36** Robert Tybetot: Undertaking to serve in the Holy Land: 1270. Paen de Chaworth: Undertaking to serve in the Holy Land: 1270 (ink on parchment), English School, (13th century) / British Library, London, UK / Bridgeman Images; **p.37** © DeAgostini / Getty Images; **p.38** © Eg 1500 f.45v Two miniatures showing Crusaders being led by Peter the Hermit, c.1095, Histoire Universelle, c.1286 (vellum) (see 11457 for detail) / British Library, London, UK / © British Library Board. All Rights Reserved / Bridgeman Images; **p.39** © Zoya Fedorova - 123rf; **p.41** © © Classic Image / Alamy Stock Photo; **p.42** © Heritage Image Partnership Ltd / Alamy Stock Photo; **p.43** © Hulton Archive / Getty Images; **pp.44–45** © DeAgostini / Getty Images; **p.46** © Museo Civico, Padua, Italy / De Agostini Picture Library / A. Dagli Orti / Bridgeman Image; **p.47** © Leemage / Corbis via Getty Images; **p.51** *t* © nejdetduzen / Getty Images, *b* © Bibliotheque Nationale, Paris, France / Getty Images; **p.52** © Universal History Archive / Getty Images; **p.53** © Heritage Image Partnership Ltd / Alamy Stock Photo; **p.54** © INTERFOTO / Alamy Stock Photo; **p.56** © Wilmar Topshots / Alamy Stock Photo; **p.58** © Universal Images Group North America LLC / DeAgostini / Alamy Stock Photo; **p.59** Armenia: Baldwin of Boulogne receiving the homage of the Armenians in Edessa (today southern Turkey). Guillaume de Tyr, 1286 / Pictures from History / Bridgeman Images; **p.60** *t* Soldiers mining under a mantlet / British Library, London, UK / © British Library Board. All Rights Reserved / Bridgeman Images, *b* © Godfrey de Bouillon's forces breach the walls of Jerusalem (gouache on paper), Nicolle, Pat (Patrick) (1907–95) / Private Collection / © Look and Learn / Bridgeman Images; **p.61** © Universal History Archive / Getty Images; **p.62** © Artokoloro Quint Lox Limited / Alamy Stock Photo; **p.65** Royal 20 C. VII, f.136v Passage of the Seine, illustration from the 'Chroniques de France ou de St. Denis' (vellum), French School, (14th century) / British Library, London, UK / © British Library Board. All Rights Reserved / Bridgeman Images; **p.66** © Ms 722/1196 f.215r Pilgrims before the statue of St. James, from Le Miroir Historial, by Vincent de Beauvais (vellum), French School, (15th century) / Musee Conde, Chantilly, France / Bridgeman Images; **p.67** © English Heritage / Heritage Images / Getty Images; **p.68** *l* © Art Collection 2 / Alamy Stock Photo, *r* © Art Collection 2 / Alamy Stock Photo; **p.69** Ms Or 20 f.19r Iskandar extends his realm into northern regions perpetually shrouded in fog, miniature from the 'Jami' al-Tawarikh' of Rashid al-Din, c.1307 (vellum), Islamic School, (14th century) / Edinburgh University Library, Scotland / With kind permission of the University of Edinburgh / Bridgeman Images; **p.70** Bohemond leading a night attack (colour litho), English School, (20th century) / Private Collection / The Stapleton Collection / Bridgeman Images; **p.72** © Keystone-France / Gamma-Keystone via Getty Images; **p.73** © Birney Lettick; **p.74** Cotton Tiberius C. VI, f.13 The Crucifixion, from the Tiberius Psalter, c.1050 (vellum), English School, (11th century) / British Library, London, UK / © British Library Board. All Rights Reserved / Bridgeman Images; **p.75** © INSADCO Photography / Alamy Stock Photo; **p.76** © Heritage Image Partnership Ltd / Alamy Stock Photo; **p.77** Yates Thompson 12 f.29 Battle scene outside Antioch, c.1098 (vellum), William of Tyre (Archbishop) (c.1130–85) / British Library, London, UK / © British Library Board. All Rights Reserved / Bridgeman Images; **p.78** © Heritage Image Partnership Ltd / Alamy Stock Photo; **p.79** *t* © D Legakis / Alamy Stock Photo, *b* © Nick Moore / Alamy Stock Photo; **p.80** © Photo 12 / Alamy Stock Photo; **p.81** © Heritage Image Partnership Ltd / Alamy Stock Photos; **p.82** © ZU_09 via Getty Images; **p.83** *t* © Art Collection 2 / Alamy Stock Photo, *m* Godfrey of Bouillon (chromolitho), French School, (19th century) / Private Collection / © Look and Learn / Bridgeman Images, *b* © Art Collection 2 / Alamy Stock Photo; **p.85** © Classic Image / Alamy Stock Photo; **pp.86–87** © whitemay – / iStockphoto; **p.88** © Sonia Halliday Photo Library / Alamy Stock Photo; **p.90** Trade card with an image of the coronation of Godefroy de Bouillon (chromolitho), French School, (19th century) / Private Collection / © Look and Learn / Bridgeman Images; **p.93** © Heritage Image Partnership Ltd / Alamy Stock Photo; **p.95** A burial. A king being crowned. / British Library, London, UK / © British Library Board. All Rights Reserved / Bridgeman Images; **p.96** © Jens Benninghofen / Alamy Stock Photo; **p.97** © Izzet Keribar / Lonely Planet Images / Getty Images; **p.103** Yates Thompson 12 f.29 Battle scene outside Antioch, c.1098 (vellum), William of Tyre (Archbishop) (c.1130 -85) / British Library, London, UK / © British Library Board. All Rights Reserved / Bridgeman Images.